"Choose Yo

Holiday

Or

Holy Day

3rd Edition

compiled by

Joy Lene'

This material is dedicated in memory of my Mom & Dad, Odessa & Orville Middleton. They gave me a loving home in which to learn about my heavenly Father and His Son. I thank them for their love of and dedication to YHWH (God of Israel) and His son Yeshua (Jesus).

I admired my Mom's persistence after my Dad passed away in seeking the truth of the Word. For many years she had known there was "more" to the Word than what she had been taught. At last, through her studies of our Hebraic Roots, she had found the doorway to the "more" she had always been searching to find. It was a great pleasure to have made the beginning of this journey with her toward the end of her life!

With fond and loving memories of my Mom and Dad,

Joy

Acknowledgements

FIRST AND FOREMOST... We (my family & I) wish to thank YHWH, our Creator, Deliverer, Redeemer, Counselor, Guide & Promise Keeper for His revelation and guidance to us through Himself, His Son, Yeshua and His Spirit, Ruach HaKodesh

We also wish to thank our many family, friends and fellow students for their prayers, time, and input during the research and study of this material. The research and dedication of many of our fellow brothers and sisters in the Hebraic study is greatly appreciated and acknowledged! We can never express our grateful appreciation for their endless study, prayer for guidance from the Ruach HaKodesh and desire to share their revelations with us and the world!

Blessings be to you all for your love of the Living Word

- *in written form: Torah, the Prophets, the Writings (The Old Testament) and the Renewed Covenant (New Testament)*
- *in the physical example of Yeshua our Messiah*
- *and in the spiritual guidance from the Set Apart Spirit, Ruach HaKodesh*

Acknowledgements

Special thanks to:

our dear friend and sister, Debra Reno, for taking the time, patience and interest to edit these pages of material,

our daughter, Kristin Torres, for her menorah artwork,

and last but not least, to my wonderful husband, Dennis, who has been so supportive of my efforts! Without his prayer and support, this material would not exist!

Preface

The following material has been compiled with research and studies in the Hebraic scriptures. These studies were brought about by our (my family & my) own questions and "stumbling" as we have tried to discover our Heavenly Father's wishes and desires for our lives and for eternity.

It is not our intent to offend anyone with this material or our presentation of it. It is our intent, through the presentation of this material, to help someone else stop and ask "WHY?"...to truly seek the Father's Way above man's.

We do stand firm in our belief in the one true God of Israel (YHWH – our Creator), His bodily form sent to earth as His Son (Yeshua - our Messiah and Savior), and His Holy Spirit (Ruach HaKodesh - our Guide and Comforter).

We pray that whoever reads this material will read it with an open heart and mind and accept it with the love with which it was written and intended. Our greatest prayer is that you, as the reader, will search the scriptures and pray for the Father's wisdom and understanding for yourself to build upon and strengthen your own personal relationship with our Creator, YHWH.

"Blessed be YHWH, our Father and Creator of all things! May YHWH through His Set Apart Spirit, Ruach HaKodesh, give you an eye to see and an ear to hear HIS Word, understand it and apply it to your own life."
Amen

Table of Contents

Table of Contents (con't)

Introduction

Don't know much about Jewish Holy Days but celebrate Christian holidays? Have never considered celebrating any of the Jewish Holy Days because they are "Jewish"? Let's dig into our roots as believers in the one true God of Israel, YHWH. Are you of Jewish/Israel decent? No? Or at least not that you know of?

That's okay, as a member of the Father's House (The House of Israel), you are accepted as an adopted child through your spiritual belief and obedience to YHWH and His earthly form Yeshua HaMassiach (or as the Christian world knows Him, Jesus the Messiah). Scripture tells us that we, whether we are "native born" or "gentile" need to have two things to be grafted into the natural olive tree:

1.) must have faith (in His promises and the saving blood of Yeshua the Messiah) and

2.) continue in the ***goodness*** of YHWH our Father.

Goodness is defined by Strong's Concordance #5544 as: *usefulness, that is, moral excellence (in character or demeanor)* {1}

The only "blood" that makes you a member of the Father's House is Yeshua's, not your fleshly ancestry.

> **(16)** And if the firstfruit is holy, so is the lump: and if the root is holy, so are the branches. **(17)** But if some of the branches (*native born*) were broken off, and thou, being a wild olive (*not native born*), wast grafted in among them, and didst become partaker with them of the root of the fatness of the olive tree; **(18)** glory not over the branches:

Introduction *(con't)*

> but if thou gloriest, it is not thou that bearest the root, but the root thee. **(19)** Thou wilt say then, Branches were broken off, that I might be grafted in. **(20)** Well; by their unbelief they were broken off, and thou standest by thy faith. Be not highminded, but fear: **(21)** for if God spared not the natural branches, neither will he spare thee. **(22)** Behold then the goodness and severity of God: toward them that fell, severity; but toward thee, God's goodness, if thou continue in his goodness: otherwise thou also shalt be cut off. **(23)** And they also, if they continue not in their unbelief, shall be grafted in: for God is able to graft them in again. **(24)** For if thou wast cut out of that which is by nature a wild olive tree, and wast grafted contrary to nature into a good olive tree; how much more shall these, which are the natural *branches*, be grafted into their own olive tree?
>
> **---Romans 11:16-24 (ASV)**

We must all "believe" to be a member of His family, the natural olive tree with Yeshua as the root!

Introduction (con't)

(28) There is neither Jew nor Greek, there is neither bond nor free, there is neither male nor female: for ye are all one in Christ Jesus. **(29)** And if ye *be* Christ's, then are ye Abraham's seed, and heirs according to the promise.

---Galatians 3:28-29 (KJV)

We belong to ONE house...
the Father's House...
the Commonwealth of Israel!

So, let's get started....

Introduction (con't)

Following is an excerpt from www.wikipedia.com for your consideration:
[People who observe the Feast of Trumpets have sometimes been subject to ridicule or condemnation.

Here is some of what the Roman Catholic saint John Chrysostom preached in 387 A.D.:

> "The festivals of the pitiful and miserable Jews are soon to march upon us one after the other and in quick succession: the feast of Trumpets, the feast of Tabernacles, the fast. There are many in our ranks who say they think as we do. Yet some of these are going to watch the festivals and others will join the Jews in keeping their feasts and observing their fasts. I wish to drive this perverse custom from the Church right now…If the Jewish ceremonies are venerable and great, ours are lies…Does God hate their festivals and do you share in them? He did not say this or that festival, but all of them together. (John Chrysostom. Homily I Against the Jews I:5; VI:5, VII:2. Preached at Antioch, Syria in the Fall of 387 AD. Medieval Sourcebook: Saint John Chrysostom (C. 347-407): Eight Homilies Against the Jews. Fordham University. http://www.fordham.edu/halsall/source/chrysostom-jews6.html 12/10/05).

John Chrysostom preached against the Fall holy days then, because some who professed Christ were observing them. It is interesting to note that he must have realized that the second century church kept Passover the same time as the Jews did (this was even true in the early second century in Rome.) And that the Catholic Church still kept Pentecost when he wrote that. Hence it is unclear why he railed against some "feasts of the Jews" and not others.

Introduction (con't)

Those who continue to observe these days do not consider that they are Jewish Feasts, but that they are biblical feast of God, citing Leviticus 23:1 where God calls them "My feasts".] {2}

to the Father's will, not man's.

As we begin this portion, please keep in mind that we believe as children of our Heavenly Father, it should be our goal to please Him. We will warn you, that if that is truly your goal, you may find (as we did) the following historical facts a little hard to swallow.

We have researched the origins of many of our Christian holidays and the Holy Days as given to mankind by our Heavenly Father. As you discover the history and origins of the holidays you observe, please ask yourself these questions, "**Would this please YHWH (God) my Heavenly Father?**" and "**What would Yeshua (Jesus) do?**" or better yet,

"What DID Yeshua (Jesus) do?"

We pray that you will read the following material with prayer for guidance and truth from the Ruach HaKodesh (the Set-Apart Spirit). After all, if we, as the children of YHWH, are going to partake in ANYTHING, we should at least know what it is and why we are doing it!

Introduction (con't)

In discussing this topic with other believers, we have run across many reasons given for celebrating what we know as "Christian" holidays:

1.) "I celebrate Christmas to remember and honor Jesus' birth."
2.) "I know Easter and Christmas were originally pagan holidays celebrated to their gods, but I observe them as Christian holidays, not pagan."
3.) "I don't put up a Christmas tree and worship it as a god."
4.) "I understand that we shouldn't celebrate Halloween if we are Christians, but I know that God knows what is in my heart when I celebrate Christmas and Easter."

In reality, our observance of these holidays stem from our upbringing. It is a cycle that started many, many years ago. The most truthful explanation for celebrating holidays is that it has been tradition or custom for our families through the years. Are they mentioned in scripture?

One of the scriptural accounts that made us stop dead in our tracks and re-think if our observing certain holidays is pleasing to YHWH was:

> **(1)** And when the people saw that Moses delayed to come down out of the mount, the people gathered themselves together unto Aaron, and said unto him, Up, make us gods, which shall go before us; for *as for* this Moses, the man that brought us up out of the land of Egypt, we wot not what is become of him.

Introduction *(con't)*

(2) And Aaron said unto them, Break off the golden earrings, which *are* in the ears of your wives, of your sons, and of your daughters, and bring *them* unto me. **(3)** And all the people brake off the golden earrings which *were* in their ears, and brought *them* unto Aaron. **(4)** And he received *them* at their hand, and fashioned it with a graving tool, after he had made it a molten calf: and they said, These *be* thy gods, O Israel, which brought thee up out of the land of Egypt. **(5)** And when Aaron saw *it*, he built an altar before it; and Aaron made proclamation, and said, To morrow *is* a feast to the LORD. **(6)** And they rose up early on the morrow, and offered burnt offerings, and brought peace offerings; and the people sat down to eat and to drink, and rose up to play. **(7)** And the LORD said unto Moses, Go, get thee down; for thy people, which thou broughtest out of the land of Egypt, have corrupted *themselves*: **(8)** They have turned aside quickly out of the way which I commanded them: they have made them a molten calf, and have worshipped it, and have sacrificed thereunto, and said, These *be* thy gods, O Israel, which have brought thee up out of the land of Egypt. **(9)** And the LORD said unto Moses, I have seen this people, and, behold, it *is* a stiffnecked people: **(10)** Now therefore let me alone, that my wrath may wax hot against them, and that I may consume them: and I will make of thee a great nation.

Introduction (con't)

(11) And Moses besought the LORD his God, and said, LORD, why doth thy wrath wax hot against thy people, which thou hast brought forth out of the land of Egypt with great power, and with a mighty hand? **(12)** Wherefore should the Egyptians speak, and say, For mischief did he bring them out, to slay them in the mountains, and to consume them from the face of the earth? Turn from thy fierce wrath, and repent of this evil against thy people. **(13)** Remember Abraham, Isaac, and Israel, thy servants, to whom thou swarest by thine own self, and saidst unto them, I will multiply your seed as the stars of heaven, and all this land that I have spoken of will I give unto your seed, and they shall inherit *it* for ever. **(14)** And the LORD repented of the evil which he thought to do unto his people. **(15)** And Moses turned, and went down from the mount, and the two tables of the testimony *were* in his hand: the tables *were* written on both their sides; on the one side and on the other *were* they written. **(16)** And the tables *were* the work of God, and the writing *was* the writing of God, graven upon the tables. **(17)** And when Joshua heard the noise of the people as they shouted, he said unto Moses, *There is* a noise of war in the camp. **(18)** And he said, *It is* not the voice of *them that* shout for mastery, neither *is it* the voice of *them that* cry for being overcome: *but* the noise of *them that* sing do I hear. **(19)** And it came to pass, as soon as he came nigh unto the camp, that he saw the calf, and the dancing: and Moses' anger waxed hot, and he cast

Introduction *(con't)*

the tables out of his hands, and brake them beneath the mount. **(20)** And he took the calf which they had made, and burnt *it* in the fire, and ground *it* to powder, and strawed *it* upon the water, and made the children of Israel drink *of it*. **(21)** And Moses said unto Aaron, What did this people unto thee, that thou hast brought so great a sin upon them? **(22)** And Aaron said, Let not the anger of my lord wax hot: thou knowest the people, that they *are set* on mischief. **(23)** For they said unto me, Make us gods, which shall go before us: for *as for* this Moses, the man that brought us up out of the land of Egypt, we wot not what is become of him. **(24)** And I said unto them, Whosoever hath any gold, let them break *it* off. So they gave *it* me: then I cast it into the fire, and there came out this calf. **(25)** And when Moses saw that the people *were* naked; (for Aaron had made them naked unto *their* shame among their enemies:) **(26)** Then Moses stood in the gate of the camp, and said, Who *is* on the LORD'S side? *let him come* unto me. And all the sons of Levi gathered themselves together unto him. **(27)** And he said unto them, Thus saith the LORD God of Israel, Put every man his sword by his side, *and* go in and out from gate to gate throughout the camp, and slay every man his brother, and every man his companion, and every man his neighbour. **(28)** And the children of Levi did according to the word of Moses: and there fell of the people that day about three thousand men. **(29)** For Moses had said, Consecrate yourselves to day to

Introduction (con't)

the LORD, even every man upon his son, and upon his
brother; that he may bestow upon you a blessing this day.
(30) And it came to pass on the morrow, that Moses said
unto the people, Ye have sinned a great sin: and now I will
go up unto the LORD; peradventure I shall make an
atonement for your sin. **(31)** And Moses returned unto the
LORD, and said, Oh, this people have sinned a great sin,
and have made them gods of gold. **(32)** Yet now, if thou
wilt forgive their sin--; and if not, blot me, I pray thee, out
of thy book which thou hast written. **(33)** And the LORD
said unto Moses, Whosoever hath sinned against me, him
will I blot out of my book. **(34)** Therefore now go, lead the
people unto *the place* of which I have spoken unto thee:
behold, mine Angel shall go before thee: nevertheless in
the day when I visit I will visit their sin upon them. **(35)**
And the LORD plagued the people, because they made the
calf, which Aaron made.

---Exodus 32:1-35 (KJV)

There is not a Christian alive that was brought up in "Sunday school" that has not heard the story of the "golden calf". Let us take a closer look....

Introduction (con't)

Moses had been up on the mountain with YHWH. The people grew restless and demanded Aaron, Moses' brother, to make them "gods". Aaron, being left in charge, gathered up their golden jewelry and created a "molten calf" of gold. Verse 4 tells us that Aaron presented the molten calf, ***"These be thy gods, O Israel, which brought thee up out of the land of Egypt."*** Knowing the character of your Heavenly Father at this point in your walk, wouldn't you have taken a few steps back from Aaron? Aaron continues by building an altar before the calf. He declares in verse 5: ***"To morrow is a feast to the LORD."***

STOP Wait a minute! He has just created this false image of a calf and declares that it will be used in a feast to the **Creator**?

When the people rose up the next morning, it was party time! Verse 6 tells us: ***"And they rose up early on the morrow, and offered burnt offerings, and brought peace offerings; and the people sat down to eat and to drink, and rose up to play."*** Verses 18 & 19 tell us that they were also singing and dancing.

Let's see what YHWH's reaction to this celebration, supposedly TO HIM, was. Verses 9 & 10: ***"And the LORD said unto Moses, I have seen this people, and, behold, it is a stiffnecked people: Now therefore let me alone, that my wrath may wax hot against them, and that I may consume them: and I will make of thee a great nation."***

Introduction (con't)

Gee, why was He so mad? After all, they were having a feast ***"unto the Lord"*** (YHWH), celebrating in His honor. As we read the remaining scriptures, we see that Moses pleads for the lives of the Israelites and the mixed multitude to be spared.

Of course, when Moses descended the mountain with the tables of stone bearing the commandments, he lost his temper and smashed the priceless tables of stone. These tablets were even written by the hand of YHWH! He then proceeds to burn the golden calf in the fire, sprinkle the remaining powder upon the water and make the children of Israel drink the water. Bet that was hard to swallow!

Then Aaron pleads for Moses not to be so angry. ***"Let not the anger of my lord wax hot: thou knowest the people, that they*** *are set* ***on mischief. For they said unto me, Make us gods, which shall go before us: for*** *as for* ***this Moses, the man that brought us up out of the land of Egypt, we wot not what is become of him. And I said unto them, Whosoever hath any gold, let them break it off. So they gave*** *it* ***me: then I cast it into the fire, and there came out this calf."*** Does anyone else find that last remark a bit humorous – "I cast it into the fire, and there came out this calf" – like "poof", magic, the calf suddenly appeared?

Verse 26 starts the decision and remaining punishments phase. Moses forces the people to make a decision as to who is on YHWH's side. Notice only the tribe of Levi comes forth.

Introduction *(con't)*

Verse 27 & 28 tell us their mission: ***"And he said unto them, Thus saith the LORD God of Israel, Put every man his sword by his side, and go in and out from gate to gate throughout the camp, and slay every man his brother, and every man his companion, and every man his neighbour. And the children of Levi did according to the word of Moses: and there fell of the people that day about three thousand men."*** These men had to be solely dedicated to pleasing their Heavenly Father in order to be able to kill their fellow brothers, companions and neighbors as commanded! Could we be that dedicated?

Moses called them to "consecrate" themselves in order that they may be blessed by YHWH. He once again goes up to the mountain to ask for forgiveness for the people. Verses 31 & 33: ***"And Moses returned unto the LORD, and said, Oh, this people have sinned a great sin, and have made them gods of gold. Yet now, if thou wilt forgive their sin--; and if not, blot me, I pray thee, out of thy book which thou hast written."*** Oh to have the heart of Moses for his fellow man! To ask for his name to be blotted out of the "book" if YHWH cannot forgive the people's sin!

YHWH answers Moses in verses 33 & 34: ***"And the LORD said unto Moses, Whosoever hath sinned against me, him will I blot out of my book. Therefore now go, lead the people unto the place of which I have spoken unto thee: behold, mine Angel shall go before thee: nevertheless in the day when I visit I will visit their sin upon them."*** We cannot imagine how the sin of His people hurt our Creator! The people had walked through the parting waters of a sea, ate manna that fell from heaven, were led by a pillar of cloud and fire, and had even heard the voice of YHWH Himself speak from a mountain relating His commandments to them. How quickly they forgot

Introduction (con't)

their God, Savior, Protector, and Provider! How much harder is it for us who have never heard or seen these things to keep our faith and not stray from His will?

Our final verse tells us that the punishment wasn't over for the people: ***"And the LORD plagued the people, because they made the calf, which Aaron made."***

It is our conclusion not only from these scriptures and this event, that our Heavenly Father is very serious about our obedience to Him. It is as one of our grandsons said: "It's His way or the highway." We see the "straight and narrow path" as His way and the "highway" as man's way.

It is our choice.

Introduction (con't)

Before we begin with the actual history and origins of our Christian holidays, let us look at one more scripture. This one was not known to us before our study!

> **(1)** Hear ye the word which the LORD speaketh to you, O house of Israel: **(2)** Thus saith the LORD, Learn not the way of the heathen, and be not dismayed at the signs of heaven; for the heathen are dismayed at them. **(3)** For the customs of the people *are* vain: for *one* cutteth a tree out of the forest, the work of the hands of the workman, with the ax. **(4)** They deck it with silver and with gold; they fasten it with nails and with hammers, that it may not move.
>
> **---Jeremiah 10:1-4 (KJV)**

Sound familiar? Verse 3 states "***customs of the people are vain***."

Vain is defined in Strong's Concordance as:

H1892 הבל הבל hebel hăbêl *heh'-bel, hab-ale'*

From H1891; ***emptiness* or *vanity***; figuratively something *transitory* (short-lived or temporary) and ***unsatisfactory***; often used as an adverb: - X altogether, vain, vanity. {1}

Introduction (con't)

We found the Strong's definition of **Idol** also interesting:

H457 אֱלִיל 'ĕlîyl *el-eel'*

Apparently from H408; good for *nothing*, by analogy ***vain* or *vanity*;** specifically an *idol:* - idol, no value, thing of nought. {1}

By the above definitions of vain, vanity and idol, this tree cut down, decked with silver and gold, fastened with nails and hammers is equal to an idol. Sobering, isn't it?

From the above definitions, ANYTHING that is good for nothing (thing of nought), vain (unsatisfactory) and of no value is considered an IDOL to YHWH. The key here is of no value and unsatisfactory to YHWH not necessarily to man! Wow, this encompasses a multitude of "things" in our modern world today!

Now, let us take a look at the definitions, history and origins of our holidays and the Father's Holy Days.

Definitions

As defined on TheFreeDictionary.com:
(Remember, these are man's definitions)

hol·i·day (hŏl'ĭ-dā')
n.
1. A day free from work that one may spend at leisure, especially a day on which custom or the law dictates a halting of general business activity to commemorate or celebrate a particular event.
2. A religious feast day; a holy day.
3. *Chiefly British* A vacation. Often used in the phrase *on holiday.*
intr.v. **holi·dayed, holi·day·ing, holi·days** *Chiefly British*
To pass a holiday or vacation. {3}

holy day also **ho·ly·day** (hō'lē-dā')
n.
A day specified for religious observance. {26}

Holy Days	Scriptural References	Date of Origin	Originator
Sabbath	*Gen 2:2-3; Ex 20:8-11, 31:12-17; Lev 23:3; Dt 5:12-15; Mt 12:1-8, 28:1; Lk 4:16; Jn 5:9; Ac 13:42; Col 2:16; Heb 4:1-11*	7th Day of Creation	**YHWH** (God of Israel)
Passover	*Ex 12:1-14; Lev 23:5; Num 9:1-14, 28:16; Dt 16:1-3a; Dt 4b-7; Mt 26:17; Mk 14:12-16; Jn 2:13, 11:55; 1 Cor 5:7; Heb 11:28*	Egypt (appr. 1447 BC)	**YHWH** (God of Israel)
Feast of Unleavened Bread	*Ex 12:15-20, 13:3-10, 23:15, 34:18; Lev 23:6-8; Num 28:17-25; Dt 16:3b; Dt 16:4a, 8; Mk 14:1, 12; Ac 12:3; 1 Cor 5:6-8*	Egypt (appr. 1447 BC)	**YHWH** (God of Israel)
Feast of Firstfruits	*Lev 23:9-14; Dt 26:5-10; Rom 8:23; 1 Cor 15:20-23*	Mt. Sinai (appr. 1447 BC)	**YHWH** (God of Israel)
Feast of Weeks	*Ex 23:16a, 34:22a; Lev 23:15-21; Num 28:26-31; Dt 16:9-12; Ac 2:1-4, 20:16; 1 Cor 16:8*	Mt. Sinai (appr. 1447 BC)	**YHWH** (God of Israel)
Feast of Trumpets	*Lev 23:23-25; Num 29:1-6*	Mt. Sinai (appr. 1447 BC)	**YHWH** (God of Israel)
Day of Atonement	*Lev 16, 23:26-32; Num 29:7-11; Rom 3:24-26; Heb 9:7, 10:3, 10:19-22*	Mt. Sinai (appr. 1447 BC)	**YHWH** (God of Israel)
Feast of Tabernacles	*Ex 23:16b,34:22b; Lev 23:33-36a, 23:39-43; Num 29:12-34; Dt 16:13-15; Zech 14:16-19; Jn 7:2, 37*	Mt. Sinai (appr. 1447 BC)	**YHWH** (God of Israel)
Feast of Dedication (Hanukkah)	*Jn 10:22; Macabees I & II*	appr. 165 BC	Israelites (note: Feast of the People, not declared by YHWH)

Holidays	Scriptural References	Date of Origin	Originator
Sunday		Constantine/321 AD	Catholicism
Epiphany		Latin/361 AD	Catholicism
Mardi Gras		arrived in US with the Le Moyne brothers/late 17th century	Catholicism
Ash Wednesday		appr 960 AD (www.americancatholic.org)	Catholicism
Lent		4th century ?	Catholicism
Valentine's Day		declared by Pope 498 AD	Catholicism
Palm Sunday		3rd or 4th century	Catholicism
St. Patrick's Day		Ireland/5th century/US 1737 AD	Catholicism
Good Friday		4th century	Catholicism
Easter	only in KJV - Acts 12:4 (Strong's defines as: G3957, pascha - Of Chaldee origin (compare [H6453]); the Passover (the meal, the day, the festival or the special sacrifices connected with it): - Easter, Passover.	Constantine-Council of Nicea/325 AD	Constantine (beginnings of Catholicism)

Holidays	***Scriptural References***	***Date of Origin***	***Originator***
Halloween		Celts/800's AD	Celts
Thanksgiving		US/1621 AD	US Pilgrams
St. Andrew's Day		Scotland/4th century?	Constantine (beginnings of Catholicism)
Christmas		Constantine-Rome/336 AD; declared a US federal holiday June 26, 1870	Constantine (beginnings of Catholicism)

History, Origins & Descriptions of Christian Holidays

Sunday

Origin Date: appr 321 AD
Originator(s): Constantine (beginning of Catholicism)
Man's Description: The first day of the week, observed as a day of rest and worship by most Christians.

[Sunday is named after *Sunne,* Germanic goddess of the sun, from which the word *sun* is also derived, although ultimately all English days names are derived from Roman or Greek mythology, in this case *dies solis,* respectively *hemera Heliou.* The practice of naming the seven days after the then known "planets" goes back to Babylonian times and was adopted by Greeks and Romans.

Sunday is considered a non-working day in many countries of the world, and are part of "the weekend". Countries predominantly influenced by Jewish or Islamic religions have Friday or Saturday as a weekly non-working day instead.

Christians from very early times have had differences of opinion on the question of whether the Sabbath should be observed on a Saturday or a Sunday. The issue does not arise for Jews, for whom the Shabbat is unquestionably on Saturday, nor for Muslims whose day of assembly (jumu'ah) is on a Friday.

Sunday (con't)

On 7 March 321, Constantine I decreed that Sunday (dies Solis) will be observed as the Roman day of rest [CJ3.12.2]:

> *On the venerable day of the Sun let the magistrates and people residing in cities rest, and let all workshops be closed. In the country however persons engaged in agriculture may freely and lawfully continue their pursuits because it often happens that another day is not suitable for grain-sowing or vine planting; lest by neglecting the proper moment for such operations the bounty of heaven should be lost.*

Though some Christians use the decree in support of the move of the Sabbath day to Sunday, in fact the decree was in support of the worship of the Sun-God (see Sol Invictus). In any event, the decree did not apply to Christians or Jews. It was part of the Roman civil law and religion and not an edict of the Church.] {17}

[The Roman Consul/Emperor **Constantine I** gave us the term ***Sun-Day***, which referred to *Sol Invictus Mithras* (the unconquerable sun, Mithras). In 321 CE he decreed under the penalty of death that all artisans, merchants, and people of his Empire cease work on the ***Venerable Day of the Sun***, to honor Mithras. This was a Universal Edict, and is still enforced in our western culture with our "blue laws". (Interestingly, the **government phone numbers** are printed on *blue pages* in our US phone books). It was a weekly ritual of sun-worshippers to assemble at dawn on this day to greet the sun at its rising. A great pillar, or sun-ray *obelisk* was the solar religion's primitive high place, condemned by Scripture as a "pillar of jealousy" ~ secretly interpreted as a male fertility symbol.

Sunday (con't)

Here's a big foundational girder with no rivets, installed by Constantine in the Roman year 321 CE. This 7th day, the commemoration of Creation in which we honor the Creator *AS* the Creator is a "Temple in time" from sunset "Frey Day" to sunset "Satyr Day" ~ changed to his "Sun-Day" under penalty of death, by only the authority of a man! All theologians and scholars admit there is no Scriptural basis for this change, but it was done by the authority of "the Church". This day which was set-apart at Creation to be a day of complete rest from work has been "superseded" by traditions that served to unite Pagans with the Nazarene sect. Constantine's historian, *Eusebius,* records the Emperor's edict: *"All things what so ever that was duty to do on the* ***Sabbath****, these* ***WE*** *have transferred to the Lord's Day"*. He also recorded Constantine's infuriated words, *"The cursed wretches who killed our Lord . . .* (the Italian Romans executed Him, Constantine's people!) . . .*We will have NOTHING in common with the hostile rabble of the Yahudim* ("Jews")". Remember, the Romans executed our Nazarene Rabbi for *sedition*, or the claim that He was a king ~ Caesar ruled as a religious king. Sabbath is the "sign" of the Everlasting Covenant, indicating who we worship.] {4}

Epiphany

Origin Date: appr 361 AD
Originator(s): Catholicism
Man's Description: *[*Epiphany is a Christian festival, observed on January 6, commemorating the manifestation of Christ to the gentiles in the persons of the Magi; Twelfth-day.] {5}

[The observance had its origins in the eastern Christian churches, and included the birth of Jesus Christ; the visit of the three Magi (Caspar, Melchior and Balthasar) who arrived in Bethlehem; and all of Jesus' childhood events, up to his baptism in the Jordan by John the Baptist.] {18}

[The Epiphany of our Lord is the wonderful liturgical festival observed on January 6. It is the oldest of the Christmas festivals and originally the most important. It is still the climax of the Christmas season in churches of the Eastern Orthodox tradition. Since January 6 is most often a weekday, Lutherans and liturgical Protestants sometimes shift the celebration of Epiphany to the Sunday immediately following the 6th. Epiphany is also a season that lasts until the beginning of Lent and encompasses four to nine Sundays, depending on the date of Easter.] {6}

[Prior to 1970, the Roman Catholic Church (and prior to 1976, the Anglican churches) reckoned Epiphany as an eight-day feast, beginning on January 6 and continuing through the Octave of Epiphany, or January 13. More recently, Roman Catholics in the United States mark Epiphany on the Sunday after the first Saturday in January (before this the Sunday between January 1 and January 6, in years when there was one, was designated the Feast of the Holy Name of Jesus), and all Catholics and Anglicans (along with many other Protestants)

Epiphany *(con't)*

now formally end the Christmas season on the Sunday immediately following January 6, or, for American Catholics, the ensuing Monday in years when the Epiphany falls on January 7 or 8. In either case, the feast of the Baptism of the Lord is observed on the latter day, after which the first installment of Ordinary Time begins.] {18}

Wow, who would have thought something that seems so simple would turn out to be so complicated?

[Today in Eastern Orthodox churches, the emphasis at this feast is on the shining forth and revelation of Jesus Christ as the Messiah and Second Person of the Trinity at the time of his baptism. It is also celebrated because, according to tradition, the baptism of Jesus in the Jordan River by St. John the Baptist marked one of only two occasions when all three Persons of the Trinity manifested themselves simultaneously to humanity: God the Father by speaking through the clouds, God the Son being baptized in the river, and God the Holy Spirit in the shape of a dove descending from heaven (the other occasion was the Transfiguration on Mount Tabor). Thus the holy day is considered to be a Trinitarian feast.] {18}

Mardi Gras

Origin Date: in US late 17th Century with the Le Moyne brothers
Originator(s): Catholicism
Man's Description: Mardi Gras means "Fat Tuesday" in French.

[Traditionally, rich foods such as eggs, meat, oils and butter were strictly prohibited during the 40 days of Lent. It thus became customary to eat all that remained of these foods in the house and enjoy one last feast on the day before the 40-day fast. One of the most well-known names for this day, ***Mardi Gras*** (French for "Fat Tuesday"), reflects the tradition of enjoying rich foods on this day.

Another common name for the holiday, **Carnival**, may also refer to this last enjoyment of rich foods. Some believe it derives from the medieval Latin *carnem levare* or *carnelevarium*, which means to take away or remove meat.

The name "**Shrove Tuesday**" derives from the practice of "shriving," or the confession and absolution of sin, that takes place on that day. According to a pre-1000 AD English *Ecclesiastical Institutes*:

> In the week immediately before Lent everyone shall go to his confessor and confess his deeds and the confessor shall so shrive him as he then may hear by his deeds what he is to do [in the way of penance].

As with many Christian holidays, the celebrations of Mardi Gras were probably adapted in some way from pagan festivals. "It possibly has its roots in a primitive festival honouring the beginning of the new year and the rebirth of nature, thought it is also possible that the beginnings of carnival in Italy may be

Mardi Gras (con't)

linked to the pagan Saturnalian festival of ancient Rome."

Today, the celebration of Mardi Gras/carnival has very little to do with religion. Although found primarily in Roman Catholic regions and based on the tradition of Shrove Tuesday, carnival is a time for raucous celebration and merrymaking to an excess that the Church frowns upon.

In earlier times, Rome was the place to be for the carnival, as its celebrations were unsurpassed in splendor. The Rome Carnival played a major role in the development of dance, theater and music. Today, the most famous Carnival celebrations take place in New Orleans, Rio de Janeiro and Venice, which include masked balls, elaborate costumes, parades and many other festivities.

Carnival celebrations vary in their length and nature throughout the world. In Munich and Bavaria, **Fasching** (as Carnival is called) begins on Epiphany (January 6), but in Cologne and the Rhineland it begins on November 11 at 11:11 AM. In France, it is celebrated only on the day before Ash Wednesday (thus Mardi Gras, "Fat Tuesday").

The New Orleans Mardi Gras celebration begins on Epiphany and ends on "Fat Tuesday". In many places, Carnival begins on Quinquagesima Sunday (the Sunday before Ash Wednesday) and ends on Shrove Tuesday.] {7}

Ash Wednesday

Origin Date:* *appr 960 AD
Originator(s): Catholicism
Man's Description: [First day of Lent, the 40-day period (not including Sundays) of fasting and repentance leading up to Easter. Up until the 7th century, Lent began on the Sunday (Quadragestima Sunday) six weeks prior to Easter, but the four extra days were eventually added to parallel Jesus' 40 days of fasting in the wilderness. The ashes used on Ash Wednesday are usually derived from burning the blessed palm branches left from the last Palm Sunday celebration. The ashes are blessed, sprinkled with holy water and fumigated with incense.

Members of the clergy receive ashes from fellow clergy, usually from the most senior member of the clergy present. Monks receive their mark of ashes on their tonsure (shaved head) rather than their foreheads. Priests then place ashes on all willing members of the congregation, usually in the shape of a cross.] {27} **(picture courtesy of www.whyeaster.com)**

…reminds us of the following scriptures:

(16) And he causeth all, the small and the great, and the rich and the poor, and the free and the bond, that there be given them a mark on their right hand, or upon their forehead; **(17)** and that no man should be able to buy or to sell, save he that hath the mark, *even* the name of the beast or the number of his name.

---Revelation 13:16-17 (ASV)

Ash Wednesday (con't)

Folks, the "he" here is the "beast"!

> **(9)** Then another angel, a third one, followed them, saying in a loud voice, "Whoever worships the beast and its image and receives a mark on his forehead or his hand **(10)** will drink the wine of God's wrath, which has been poured undiluted into the cup of his anger. He will be tortured with fire and sulfur in the presence of the holy angels and the lamb. **(11)** The smoke from their torture goes up forever and ever. There is no rest day or night for those who worship the beast and its image or for anyone who receives the mark of its name."
>
> **---Revelation 14:9-11 (ISV)**

Notice the Paleo Hebrew symbol for the English word "mark" as taken from Lew White's "*Fossilized Customs*" book: (entire table on next page)

Latin Symbol	Hebrew Name	Paleo	Modern	Gematria	Meaning	Greek Name	Greek
T	**tau**	×	ת	400	mark	**tau**	T

HEBREW {4}

LATIN SYMBOL	HEBREW NAME	PALAEO	MODERN	GEMATRIA	MEANING	GREEK NAME	GREEK
A	alef	𐤀	א	1	ox	alpha	A
B	beth	𐤁	ב	2	house	beta	B
G	gimel	𐤂	ג	3	camel	gamma	Γ
D	daleth	𐤃	ד	4	door	delta	Δ
H	hay	𐤄	ה	5	window	hoi	H
W	waw	𐤅	ו	6	hook	digamma	F
Z	zayin	𐤆	ז	7	weapon	zeta	Z
CH	heth	𐤇	ח	8	fence	(h)eta	H
T	teth	𐤈	ט	9	winding	theta	Θ
Y	yod	𐤉	י	10	hand	iota	I
K	kaph	𐤊	כ	20	bent hand	kappa	K
L	lamed	𐤋	ל	30	goad	lambda	Λ
M	mem	𐤌	מ	40	water	mu	M
N	nun	𐤍	נ	50	fish	nu	N
S	samek	𐤎	ס	60	prop	xei	Ξ
-	ayin	𐤏	ע	70	eye	omega	Ω
P	pe	𐤐	פ	80	mouth	pei	Π
TZ	tsadee	𐤑	צ	90	hook	zeta	Z
Q	koph	𐤒	ק	100	needle eye	chi	X
R	resh	𐤓	ר	200	head	rho	P
SH	shin	𐤔	שׁ	300	tooth	sigma	Σ
T	tau	𐤕	ת	400	mark	tau	T

"…but as for me and my house, we will serve the LORD (YHVH)"
Joshua 24:15

Lent

Origin Date: 4th Century
Originator(s): Catholicism
Man's Description: [Lent (also called the **Lenten Season**) is a 40-day period of fasting and repentance in preparation for the celebration of Easter.

It has been observed since apostolic times as a period of reflection and penitence for those who would be baptized on Easter, and a time for all sinners to repent.

Lent was originally observed for six weeks excluding Sundays (36 days), but this was eventually extended to 40 days in order to parallel Christ's temptation in the wilderness. In the Western Churches, Lent begins on Ash Wednesday (six and a half weeks before Easter).

In the early history of the church, strict fasting was observed throughout this period. One meal was allowed per day, in the evening, and meat, fish, eggs, and butter were forbidden. Strict observance of fasting was discontinued among Roman Catholics during World War II, and today is rarely observed throughout the Lenten Season.

However, Ash Wednesday and Good Friday are still fast days for the Catholic Church, and the emphasis on Lent as a period of penitence remains. Many Christians, especially Catholics, choose to give up a single indulgence (like chocolate, french fries or cola) for the 40-day period as a sign of repentance and an exercise in self-control.

Eastern Churches continue to observe a strict fast during "Great Lent," which begins on the Monday of the seventh week before Easter and ends on the Friday preceding Good

Lent (con't)

Friday. As in the early church, meat, fish, eggs, and butter are forbidden, as are wine, oil, and dairy products.] {28}

[The word lent simply means spring, but commonly refers to a long period of abstinence. In the Babylonian myth, Tammuz was killed by a wild boar, and his wife Ishtar dedicated 40 days to weeping and fasting.] {8}

> **(14)** Then he brought me to the entrance of the gate to the LORD's Temple, which faced the north. That's where I saw women seated, weeping for Tammuz.

---Ezekiel 8:14 (ISV)

Valentine's Day

Origin Date: declared by Pope 496 AD
Originator(s): Catholicism
Man's Description: In Ancient Rome, February 15 was Lupercalia.

[Valentine's Day is a celebration of romantic love occurring annually on February 14.

Although it is associated by legend with a Catholic saint named Valentine, Valentine's Day is not a religious holiday and never really has been. Valentine's Day has historical roots mainly in Greco-Roman pagan fertility festivals and the medieval notion that birds pair off to mate on February 14.

The association of the middle of February with love and fertility dates to ancient times. In ancient Athens, the period between mid-January and mid-February was the month of Gamelion, which was dedicated to the sacred marriage of Zeus and Hera.

In ancient Rome, February 15 was **Lupercalia**, the festival of Lupercus (or Faunus), the god of fertility. As part of the purification ritual, the priests of Lupercus would sacrifice goats and a dog to the god, and after drinking wine, they would run through the streets of Rome striking anyone they met with pieces of the goat skin. Young women would come forth voluntarily for the occasion, believing that being touched by the goat skin would render them fertile. Young men would also draw names from an urn, choosing their "blind date" for the coming year. In 494 AD the Christian church under Pope Gelasius I appropriated the same aspects of the rite as the Feast of the Purification.

Valentine's Day (con't)

In Christianity, at least three different **saints named Valentine** or Valentinus, all of them martyrs, are mentioned in the early lives of the saints under the date of February 14. Two of the Valentines lived in Italy in the third century: one as a priest at Rome, the other as bishop of Terni. They are both said to have been martyred in Rome and buried on the Flaminian Way. A third St. Valentine was martyred in North Africa and very little else is known of him.

Several legends have developed around one or more of these Valentines, two of which are especially popular. According to one account, Emperor Claudius II outlawed marriage for all young men because he believed unmarried men made better soldiers. Valentine defied Claudius and continued to perform marriages for young couples and was put to death by the emperor for it. A related legend has Valentine writing letters from prison to his beloved, signing them "From your Valentine."

However, the connection between St. Valentine and romantic love is not mentioned in any early histories and is regarded by historians as purely a matter of legend. The **feast of St.** Valentine was first declared to be on February 14 by Pope Gelasius I around 498. It is said the pope created the day to counter the practice held on Lupercalia, but this is not attested in any sources from that era.

The first recorded association of St. Valentine's Day with romantic love was in the 14th century in England and France, where it was believed that February 14 was the day on which **birds paired off to mate**. Thus we read in Geoffrey Chaucer's (c. 1343-1400) *Parliament of Fowls*, believed to be the first Valentine's Day poem:

Valentine's Day (con't)

For this was on Saint Valentine's Day,
When every fowl comes there to choose his mate

It became common during that era for lovers to exchange notes on Valentine's Day and to call each other their "Valentines." The **first Valentine card** was sent by Charles, duke of Orleans, to his wife in 1415 when he was a prisoner in the Tower of London. Valentine's Day love notes were often given anonymously. It is probable that many of the legends about St. Valentine developed during this period (see above). By the 1700s, verses like "Roses are red, violets are blue" became popular. By the 1850s, romantics in France began embellishing their valentine cards with gilt paper, ribbons and lace.

Valentine's Day was probably imported into North America in the 19th century with settlers from Britain. In the United States, the first **mass-produced valentines** of embossed paper lace were produced and sold shortly after 1847 by Esther A. Howland (1828 - 1904) of Worcester, Massachusetts. Her father operated a large book and stationery store, and she took her inspiration from an English valentine she had received.

In the 19th century, **relics of St. Valentine** were donated by Pope Gregory XVI to the Whitefriar Street Carmelite Church in Dublin, Ireland, which has become a popular place of pilgrimage on February 14.

But in 1969, as part of a larger effort to pare down the number of saint days of legendary origin, the Church removed St. Valentine's Day as an official holiday from its calendar.

The primary custom associated with St. Valentine's Day is the mutual exchange of love notes called **valentines**. Common

Valentine's Day (con't)

symbols on valentines are hearts, the colors red and pink, and the figure of the winged Cupid.

Starting in the 19th century, the practice of hand writing notes began to give way to the exchange of mass-produced **greeting cards**. These cards are no longer given just to lovers, but also to friends, family, classmates and coworkers. Valentine cards are often accompanied by **tiny candy hearts** with affectionate messages printed on them.

The Greeting Card Association estimates that approximately one billion valentine cards are sent worldwide each year, making Valentine's Day the second largest card-sending holiday of the year, behind Christmas. The association also estimates that women purchase approximately 85 percent of all valentines.

In the last 50 years or so, especially in the United States, the practice of exchanging cards has been extended to include the giving of **gifts**, usually from a man to his girlfriend or wife. The most popular Valentine's Day gifts are **roses** and **chocolate**. Starting in the 1980s, the diamond industry began to promote Valentine's Day as an occasion for the giving of fine jewelry. Many couples also schedule a romantic dinner date on Valentine's Day.] {29}

Palm Sunday

Origin Date: 3rd or 4th Century
Originator(s): Catholicism
Man's Description: [Palm Sunday is the sixth Sunday of Lent and the last Sunday before Easter. It is also known as Passion Sunday, Willow Sunday, and Flower Sunday.

Palm Sunday commemorates the triumphal entry of Jesus into Jerusalem, where he would be crucified five days later. According to the Gospels, Jesus rode into town on a donkey as exuberant crowds hailed him as the Messiah and spread out palm branches and cloaks in his path.

The event commemorated on Palm Sunday is told in all four gospels (Matthew 21, Mark 11, Luke 19, John 12). The Matthew narrative, the one most commonly read in services on Palm Sunday, tells the story this way:

> *As they approached Jerusalem and came to Bethphage on the Mount of Olives, Jesus sent two disciples, saying to them, "Go to the village ahead of you, and at once you will find a donkey tied there, with her colt by her. Untie them and bring them to me. If anyone says anything to you, tell him that the Lord needs them, and he will send them right away...*
>
> *The disciples went and did as Jesus had instructed them. They brought the donkey and the colt, placed their cloaks on them, and Jesus sat on them. A very large crowd spread their cloaks on the road, while others cut branches from the trees and spread them on the road.*
>
> *The crowds that went ahead of him and those that followed shouted, "Hosanna to the Son of David!*

Palm Sunday (con't)

> *Blessed is he who comes in the name of the Lord! Hosanna in the highest!"*
>
> *When Jesus entered Jerusalem, the whole city was stirred and asked, "Who is this?" the crowds answered, "This is Jesus, the prophet from Nazareth in Galillee." (Matthew 21:1-3, 6-11)*

The celebration of Palm Sunday probably originated in the churches of Jerusalem, sometime before the third or fourth century AD.

Palm Sunday marks the beginning of Holy Week, an especially solemn and important week in the Christian calendar that focuses on the last days of Jesus' life and anticipates Easter, the most important holiday in Christianity.

Common Palm Sunday observances include processions with palm branches, the blessing of palms (which will be burned and used on Ash Wednesday), and the construction of small palm crosses. Bible readings for the "Liturgy of the Palms" usually include Matthew 21:1-11 and Psalm 118:19-29.] {30}

St. Patrick's Day

***Origin Date:** appr 5th Century; US observance 1737*
Originator(s): Catholicism
Man's Description: [St. Patrick's Day is the Roman Catholic feast day that honors St. Patrick (387-461 AD), the patron saint of Ireland. Because of St. Patrick's patronage, St. Patrick's Day (**March 17**) has come to be closely associated with Ireland and Irish culture.

Since the earliest centuries of Christianity, it has been a custom to celebrate the anniversary of saints' deaths. This allows believers to honor the saint's accomplishments and celebrate their entry into heaven. A "feast day" is designated for every saint, even when the exact date of death of a saint is not known.

St. Patrick was a fifth-century English (or perhaps Scottish) missionary to Ireland. Scholars agree he is a historical figure and that he converted many of the pagans on the island to Christianity, but dismiss most of the legend that has developed about him over the centuries.

The feast day of St. Patrick has been observed in Ireland on March 17 for hundreds of years. The date falls during the fasting season of Lent, but on St. Patrick's Day the prohibitions against eating meat were lifted, and the Irish would celebrate their patron saint with dancing, drinking, and feasting on the traditional meal of Irish bacon and cabbage.

One of the most widespread of today's St. Patrick's Day celebrations, the St. Patrick's Day parade, began not in Ireland but in America. It consisted of Irish soldiers serving in the English army and took place in New York City on March 17, 1762.

St. Patrick's Day (con't)

The parade helped the soldiers connect with their Irish roots and their fellow Irishmen.

Irish patriotism flourished in America over the next several decades. Several "Irish Aid" societies were founded, each of which would hold annual parades featuring Irish music. In 1848, several Irish Aid societies in New York decided to combine their parades into a single St. Patrick's Day Parade. This parade is the oldest and the largest civilian parade.

Today, Irish expatriates, those of Irish descent, and ever-growing crowds of people with no Irish connections whatsoever celebrate St. Patrick's Day. *(see #4, page 43)*

Many Irish people wear a bunch of shamrock on their lapels or caps on St. Patrick's Day, while children wear tricolored (green, white and orange) badges. Girls traditionally wore green ribbons in their hair (many still do).

Unlike its American counterpart, St. Patrick's Day in Ireland has primarily been a religious festival. Until the 1970s, pubs were required by law to close on March 17. However, since 1995 the Irish government has sought to make St. Patrick's Day an opportunity to showcase Ireland and Irish culture to the world.

The St. Patrick's Day celebrations in Dublin have thus been extended to a week-long event called St. Patrick's Festival, encompassing a spectacular fireworks display (Skyfest), open-air music, street theater and the traditional parade. Over one million people attended the celebrations in 2004.

St. Patrick's Day is celebrated worldwide by the Irish, those of

St. Patrick's Day (con't)

Irish descent, and everyone else who enjoys being "Irish for a day." A major parade takes place in Dublin and in most other Irish towns and villages. The three largest parades of recent years have been held in Dublin, New York and Birmingham England. Parades also take place in other centers, London, Paris, Rome, Moscow, Beijing, Hong Kong, Singapore and throughout the Americas.

The New York celebration is the oldest and largest St. Patrick's Day Parade in the world. The parade dates back to 1762, and in 2003 more than 150,000 marchers (bands, military and police groups, county associations, emigrant societies, social and cultural clubs etc.) participated.

As might be expected in such a large event, it has also been dogged with controversy. Its organizers have banned Irish gays and lesbians from marching as a group, an act which has led to calls in Ireland (which, since 1992 has some of the most liberal gay laws in the world) for its boycotting. In addition, the Ancient Order of Hibernians has on occasion appointed controversial Irish Republican figures (some of whom were barred from the US) to be its Grand Marshal.

The longest running St. Patrick's Day parade in Canada takes place in Montreal. The 2003 parade was the 179th - the first Montreal parade taking place in 1824.

The most common traditions on St. Patrick's Day include wearing green, enjoying Irish folk music and food, and by consuming large quantities of Irish beer (sometimes dyed green), such as Murphys, Smithwicks, Harp or Guinness or other Irish liquors such as Irish whiskey, Irish Coffee or Baileys Irish Cream.

St. Patrick's Day (con't)

In the United States, St. Patrick's Day would not be St. Patrick's Day unless the Chicago River is dyed green. This tradition began in 1962, when Chicago pollution-control workers used green dye to trace illegal sewage discharges in the river. The workers thought it might be a fun way to celebrate St. Patrick's Day, so they released 100 pounds of green vegetable dye into the river – enough to keep it green for a week! The idea was a hit, and continues to this day. However, only 40 pounds of dye are used today to minimize environmental damage.] {32}

So much for the ecosystem!

[Since the 1990s, Irish taoisigh (prime ministers) have attended special functions either on St. Patrick's Day or a day or two earlier, in the White House, where they present shamrock to the President of the United States. A similar presentation is made to the Speaker of the House. Originally only representatives of the Republic of Ireland attended, but since the mid-1990's all major Irish political parties from north and south are invited, with the attendance including the representatives of the Irish government, the Ulster Unionists, the Social Democratic and Labour Party, Sinn Féin and others.

In recent years it is common for the entire Irish Government to be abroad representing the country in various parts of the world. In 2003, the President of Ireland celebrated the holiday in Sydney, the Taoiseach (Prime Minister) was in Washington, while other Irish government members attended ceremonies in New York, Boston, San Francisco, San Jose, Savannah, Chicago, Philadelphia, San Diego, New Zealand, Hong Kong, South Africa, Korea, Japan and Brazil.

St. Patrick's Day (con't)

In Britain, the late Queen Elizabeth, the Queen Mother used to present bowls of shamrock specially flown over from Ireland to members of the Irish Guards, a regiment in the British Army made up of Irish people from both Northern Ireland and the Republic of Ireland.

Traditional Symbols of St. Patrick's Day:
Shamrocks
According to Christian legend, St. Patrick used the three-leafed clover to illustrate the doctrine of the Trinity to his pagan audience in Ireland. However, this story did not appear until more than 1000 years after St. Patrick's death.

In ancient Ireland, the Celtic people revered the shamrock as a sacred plant because it symbolized the rebirth of spring. By the 17th century, when the English began to seize Irish land and suppress Irish language and religion, the shamrock became a symbol of Irish nationalism.

Leprechauns
The diminutive creatures we know as leprechauns were known in ancient Irish as "lobaircin," meaning "small-bodied fellow." Belief in leprechauns probably stems from Celtic belief in fairies, tiny creatures who could use their magical powers for good or evil. In Celtic folklore, the lobaircin were cranky fairies who mended the shoes of the other fairies. They were also mischievous and delighted in trickery, which they used to guard their fabled treasure.

The cheerful friendly version of the leprechaun known to us today is based in large part on Walt Disney's 1959 film *Darby O'Gill and the Little People*. It quickly evolved into a symbol of St. Patrick's Day and Ireland in general.

St. Patrick's Day (con't)

Corned Beef and Cabbage

Corned beef and cabbage is the traditional meal enjoyed by many on St. Patrick's Day, but only half of it is truly Irish. Cabbage has long been a staple of the Irish diet, but it was traditionally served with Irish bacon, not corned beef. The corned beef was substituted for bacon by Irish immigrants to the Americas around the turn of the century who could not afford the real thing. They learned about the cheaper alternative from their Jewish neighbors.] {32}

Easter

Origin Date: ***appr 325 AD***
Originator(s): Constantine-Council of Nicea (beginnings of Catholicism
Man's Description: [Easter is a spring festival that celebrates the central event of the Christian faith: the resurrection of Christ three days after his death by crucifixion. Easter is the oldest Christian holiday and the most important day of the church year. All the Christian movable feasts and the entire liturgical year of worship are arranged around Easter.

Easter Sunday is preceded by the season of Lent, a 40-day period of fasting and repentance culminating in Holy Week, and followed by a 50-day Easter Season that stretches from Easter to Pentecost.

The origins of the word "Easter" are not certain, but probably derive from Estre, an Anglo-Saxon goddess of spring. The German word *Ostern* has the same derivation, but most other languages follow the Greek term used by the early Christians: *pascha*, from the Hebrew *pesach* (Passover).] {31}

[The name Easter, like the names of the days of the week, is a survival from the old Teutonic mythology. According to Bede (an eighth century monk) it is derived from *Oestre*, or *Ostdra*, the Anglo-Saxon goddess of spring, to whom the month answering to our April, and called Eoster-monath, was dedicated.

-- "Easter", Encyclopedia Britannica, 11th ed.

Easter (con't)

What means the term Easter itself? It is not a Christian name. Easter is nothing else than Astarte, one of the titles of Beltis, the queen of heaven, whose name, as pronounced by the people of Nineveh, was evidently identical with that now in common use in this country. That name, as found by Layard on the Assyrian monuments is Ishtar."

-- The Two Babylons, Hislop, p. 103

Many ancient cultures share this legend of Semiramus and Nimrod: called by such names as Ishtar and Tammuz in Babylon; Isis and Osiris in Egypt; Astarte and Bel in Syria; Aphrodite, Cybele, or Venus, and Attis or Adonis in Greece and Rome; and Oestre (the dawn goddess) in Britain.

They considered her "the Mother of Gods", and often depicted her either as a fertility symbol, or as a madonna figure.

Many pre-christian Europeans thought that their sun gods and fertility goddesses died at the winter solstice and regained life again at the spring equinox.

Ancient Babylonians believed that Ishtar hatched from an egg that fell from heaven.
... the egg as a symbol of fertility and of renewed life goes back to the ancient Egyptians and Persians, who had also the custom of colouring and eating eggs during their spring festival.

-- "Easter", Encyclopedia Britannica, 11th ed.] {8}

[Should Christians use the 'E' word? What does the term Easter mean? In the Old Testament times the Bible talks about Ashtoreth and Baal worship in I Kings 11:5-6, "For Solomon went after Ashtoreth [Easter in English] the goddess of the

Easter *(con't)*

Zidonians, and after Milcom the abomination of the Ammonites. And Solomon did evil in the sight of the LORD, and went not fully after the LORD, as did David his father." Ashtoreth is the mother of Baal. The short form is Ashtar or Ishtar and the English form of the word is "EASTER". Easter is nothing other than the mother of Baal and the celebration or worship of Ashtoreth is forbidden in the Old Testament Scriptures. Look at the Scriptures in Judges 2:13-14, "And they forsook the LORD, and served Baal and Ashtoroth. And the anger of the LORD was hot against Israel..." Easter is Ashtoreth! EASTER IS AN EVIL WOMAN!] {9}

> **(33)** because that they have forsaken me, and have worshipped Ashtoreth the goddess of the Sidonians, Chemosh the god of Moab, and Milcom the god of the children of Ammon; and they have not walked in my ways, to do that which is right in mine eyes, and *to keep* my statutes and mine ordinances, as did David his father.

---1Kings 11:33 (ASV)

Let's see if you can understand how the "date" of Easter is determined...

[The method for determining the date of Easter is complex and has been a matter of controversy (see History of Easter, below). Put as simply as possible, the Western churches (Catholic and Protestant) celebrate Easter on the first Sunday following the first full moon after the spring equinox.

Easter *(con't)*

But it is actually a bit more complicated than this. The spring equinox is fixed for this purpose as March 21 (in 2004, it actually falls on March 20) and the "full moon" is actually the paschal moon, which is based on 84-year "paschal cycles" established in the sixth century, and rarely corresponds to the astronomical full moon. These complex calculations yield an Easter date of anywhere between March 22 and April 25.

The Eastern churches (Greek, Russian, and other forms of Orthodoxy) use the same calculation, but based on the Julian calendar (on which March 21 is April 3) and a 19-year paschal cycle.

Thus the Orthodox Easter sometimes falls on the same day as the western Easter (it does in 2004), but the two celebrations can occur as much as five weeks apart.

In the 20th century, discussions began as to a possible worldwide agreement on a consistent date for the celebration of the central event of Christianity. No resolution has yet been reached.

There is evidence that Christians originally celebrated the resurrection of Christ every Sunday, with observances such as Scripture readings, psalms, the Eucharist, and a prohibition against kneeling in prayer. At some point in the first two centuries, however, it became customary to celebrate the resurrection specially on one day each year. Many of the religious observances of this celebration were taken from the Jewish Passover.

The specific day on which the resurrection should be celebrated became a major point of contention within the

Easter *(con't)*

church. First, should it be on Jewish Passover no matter on what day that falls, or should it always fall on a Sunday? It seems Christians in Asia took the former position, while those everywhere else insisted on the latter. The eminent church fathers Irenaeus and Polycarp were among the Asiatic Christians, and they claimed the authority of St. John the Apostle for their position. Nevertheless, the church majority officially decided that Easter should always be celebrated on a Sunday. Eusebius of Caesarea, our only source on this topic, reports the affair as follows:

> "'*A question of no small importance arose at that time [c. 190 AD]. The dioceses of all Asia, as from an older tradition, held that the fourteenth day of the moon, on which day the Jews were commanded to sacrifice the lamb, should always be observed as the feast of the life-giving pasch, contending that the fast ought to end on that day, whatever day of the week it might happen to be. However it was not the custom of the churches in the rest of the world to end it at this point, as they observed the practice, which from Apostolic tradition has prevailed to the present time, of terminating the fast on no other day than on that of the Resurrection of our Saviour. Synods and assemblies of bishops were held on this account, and all with one consent through mutual correspondence drew up an ecclesiastical decree that the mystery of the Resurrection of the Lord should be celebrated on no other day but the Sunday and that we should observe the close of the paschal fast on that day only.*"] {10} {31}

Anyone else confused yet? But wait, it gets more confusing...

Easter (con't)

[With this issue resolved, the next problem was to determine *which* Sunday to celebrate the resurrection. The Christians in Syria and Mesopotamia held their festival on the Sunday after the Jewish Passover (which itself varied a great deal), but those in Alexandria and other regions held it on the first Sunday after the spring equinox, without regard to the Passover.

This second issue was decided at the Council of Nicea in 325, which decreed that Easter should be celebrated by all on the same Sunday, which Sunday shall be the first following the paschal moon (and the paschal moon must not precede the spring equinox), and that a particular church should determine the date of Easter and communicate it throughout the empire (probably Alexandria, with their skill in astronomical calculations).

The policy was adopted throughout the empire, but Rome adopted an 84-year lunar cycle for determining the date, whereas Alexandria used a 19-year cycle. Use of these different "paschal cycles" persists to this day and contributes to the disparity between the eastern and western dates of Easter.] {31}

Halloween

Origin Date: appr 800's AD
Originator(s): Celts
Description: [The modern holiday of Halloween has its origins in the ancient Gaelic festival known as Samhain (pronounced /s^{y}aun^{j}/ from the Old Irish *samain*). The festival of Samhain is a celebration of the end of the harvest season in Gaelic culture, and is sometimes erroneously regarded as the "Celtic New Year". Traditionally, the festival was a time used by the ancient pagans to take stock of supplies and slaughter livestock for winter stores. The ancient Gaels believed that on October 31, the boundaries between the worlds of the living and the dead overlapped and the deceased would come back to life and cause havoc such as sickness or damaged crops. The festivals would frequently involve bonfires, where the bones of slaughtered livestock were thrown. Costumes and masks were also worn at the festivals in an attempt to mimic the evil spirits or placate them.

The term *Halloween* (and its alternative rendering *Hallowe'en*) is shortened from **All-hallow-even**, as it is the eve of "All Hallows' Day", which is now also known as All Saints' Day. It was a day of religious festivities in various northern European Pagan traditions, until Popes Gregory III and Gregory IV moved the old Christian feast of All Saints' Day from May 13 (which had itself been the date of a pagan holiday, the Feast of Lemures) to November 1. In the ninth century, the Church measured the day as starting at sunset, in accordance with the Florentine calendar. Although All Saints' Day is now considered to occur one day after Halloween, the two holidays were, at that time, celebrated on the same day.

Liturgically, the Church traditionally celebrated that day as the Vigil of All Saints, and, until 1970, a day of fasting as well.

Halloween (*con't*)

Like other vigils, it was celebrated on the previous day if it fell on a Sunday, although secular celebrations of the holiday remained on the 31st. The Vigil was suppressed in 1955, but was later restored in the post-Vatican II calendar.

Halloween did not become a holiday in the United States until the 19th century, where lingering Puritan tradition restricted the observance of many holidays. American almanacs of the late 18th and early 19th centuries do not include Halloween in their lists of holidays. The transatlantic migration of nearly two million Irish following the Irish Potato Famine (1845-1849) finally brought the holiday to the United States. Scottish emigration, primarily to Canada before 1870 and to the United States thereafter, brought the Scottish version of the holiday to each country.

Halloween is now the United States' second most popular holiday (after Christmas) for decorating; the sale of candy and costumes are also extremely common during the holiday, which is marketed to children and adults alike. According to the National Retail Federation, the most popular Halloween costume themes for adults are, in order: witch, pirate, vampire, cat and clown. Each year, popular costumes are dictated by various current events and pop culture icons. On many college campuses, Halloween is a major celebration, with the Friday and Saturday nearest October 31 hosting many costume parties.] {19}

This gives honor and glory to our Savior and Creator?

[(Source material from YNCA,) The two Celtic words *Hallowed Evening* came from ***All Hallowed's Ev'n***, and now we call it "Halloween". This is now even more popular than

Halloween *(con't)*

Easter, and rivals Christmas. The roots of this festival come to us from Druid demon worship. Witches were said to fly brooms over the crops to "teach" them how to grow. It was a fertility myth.

When the first Roman Catholic missionaries encountered these Druids, they met stubborn resistance because the inhabitants of Angle Land, Sweden, Neder Land, northern Germany, Fin Land, and Eire Land were very nationalistic. The ritual we embrace as Halloween was originally called the Feast of the Dead, ***Samhain*** (pronounced *Sa-ween*), and was on November 1st. These pre-Christian Druids had the barbarians doing ghastly things. It was a dreaded occasion, since it was thought that time stood still, and the souls of the dead walked the land. Gifts, especially food, were left outside for these roaming ghosts, with the hope that no harm would come to the households. The Druids chose certain children to be burned alive on "bone-fires", as offerings to the sun. Parents tied yellow ribbons around oak trees as prayers to the sun to have their children spared. The fat left over from the child was fashioned into a candle, and placed into a carved-out pumpkin, or a hollowed out vegetable with a "round" (sun-shaped) design. The victim was called *Jack-of-the-lantern.* Prisoners and unliked people were burned alive in wicker cages shaped in the form of animals, hung from trees. All of this was ultimately to pay homage to the sun, *Woden,* or *Odin.* As you now know, this Druid deity gives us our name for the 4th day of the week: *Woden's Day.*] {4}

Thanksgiving

Origin Date:* *in US 1621
Originator(s): US Pilgrims
Man's Description: A national holiday in the United States and Canada celebrating the harvest and other blessings of the past year.

[During the American Revolutionary War the Continental Congress appointed one or more thanksgiving days each year, each time recommending to the executives of the various states the observance of these days in their states. The First National Proclamation of Thanksgiving was given by the Continental Congress in 1777:

> "FOR AS MUCH as it is the indispensable Duty of all Men to adore the superintending Providence of Almighty God; to acknowledge with Gratitude their Obligation to him for Benefits received, and to implore such farther Blessings as they stand in Need of: And it having pleased him in his abundant Mercy, not only to continue to us the innumerable Bounties of his common Providence; but also to smile upon us in the Prosecution of a just and necessary War, for the Defense and Establishment of our unalienable Rights and Liberties; particularly in that he hath been pleased, in so great a Measure, to prosper the Means used for the Support of our Troops, and to crown our Arms with most signal success:
>
> It is therefore recommended to the legislative or executive Powers of these UNITED STATES to set apart THURSDAY, the eighteenth Day of December next, for SOLEMN THANKSGIVING and PRAISE: That at one Time and with one Voice, the good People

Thanksgiving (con't)

may express the grateful Feelings of their Hearts, and consecrate themselves to the Service of their Divine Benefactor; and that, together with their sincere Acknowledgments and Offerings, they may join the penitent Confession of their manifold Sins, whereby they had forfeited every Favor; and their humble and earnest Supplication that it may please GOD through the Merits of JESUS CHRIST, mercifully to forgive and blot them out of Remembrance; That it may please him graciously to afford his Blessing on the Governments of these States respectively, and prosper the public Council of the whole: To inspire our Commanders, both by Land and Sea, and all under them, with that Wisdom and Fortitude which may render them fit Instruments, under the Providence of Almighty GOD, to secure for these United States, the greatest of all human Blessings, INDEPENDENCE and PEACE: That it may please him, to prosper the Trade and Manufactures of the People, and the Labor of the Husbandman, that our Land may yield its Increase: To take Schools and Seminaries of Education, so necessary for cultivating the Principles of true Liberty, Virtue and Piety, under his nurturing Hand; and to prosper the Means of Religion, for the promotion and enlargement of that Kingdom, which consisteth "in Righteousness, Peace and Joy in the Holy Ghost.

And it is further recommended, That servile Labor, and such Recreation, as, though at other Times innocent, may be unbecoming the Purpose of this Appointment, be omitted on so solemn an Occasion."

Thanksgiving (con't)

George Washington, leader of the revolutionary forces in the American Revolutionary War, , proclaimed a Thanksgiving in December 1777 as a victory celebration honoring the defeat of the British at Saratoga.

As President, on October 3, 1789, George Washington made the following proclamation and created the first Thanksgiving Day designated by the national government of the United States of America:

> "Whereas it is the duty of all Nations to acknowledge the providence of Almighty God, to obey his will, to be grateful for his benefits, and humbly to implore his protection and favor, and whereas both Houses of Congress have by their joint Committee requested me "to recommend to the People of the United States a day of public thanksgiving and prayer to be observed by acknowledging with grateful hearts the many signal favors of Almighty God especially by affording them an opportunity peaceably to establish a form of government for their safety and happiness.
>
> Now therefore I do recommend and assign Thursday the 26th day of November next to be devoted by the People of these States to the service of that great and glorious Being, who is the beneficent Author of all the good that was, that is, or that will be. That we may then all unite in rendering unto him our sincere and humble thanks, for his kind care and protection of the People of this Country previous to their becoming a Nation, for the signal and manifold mercies, and the favorable interpositions of his providence, which we experienced in the course and conclusion of the late war, for the

Thanksgiving (con't)

great degree of tranquility, union, and plenty, which we have since enjoyed, for the peaceable and rational manner, in which we have been enabled to establish constitutions of government for our safety and happiness, and particularly the national One now lately instituted, for the civil and religious liberty with which we are blessed; and the means we have of acquiring and diffusing useful knowledge; and in general for all the great and various favors which he hath been pleased to confer upon us.

And also that we may then unite in most humbly offering our prayers and supplications to the great Lord and Ruler of Nations and beseech him to pardon our national and other transgressions, to enable us all, whether in public or private stations, to perform our several and relative duties properly and punctually, to render our national government a blessing to all the people, by constantly being a Government of wise, just, and constitutional laws, discreetly and faithfully executed and obeyed, to protect and guide all Sovereigns and Nations (especially such as have shown kindness unto us) and to bless them with good government, peace, and concord. To promote the knowledge and practice of true religion and virtue, and the increase of science among them and Us, and generally to grant unto all Mankind such a degree of temporal prosperity as he alone knows to be best.

Given under my hand at the City of New York the third day of October in the year of our Lord 1789."

George Washington again proclaimed a Thanksgiving in 1795.

Thanksgiving (con't)

President John Adams declared Thanksgivings in 1798 and 1799. No Thanksgiving proclamations were issued by Thomas Jefferson but James Madison renewed the tradition in 1814, in response to resolutions of Congress, at the close of the War of 1812. Madison also declared the holiday twice in 1815; however, none of these were celebrated in autumn.

A thanksgiving day was annually appointed by the governor of New York from 1817. In some of the Southern states there was opposition to the observance of such a day on the ground that it was a relic of Puritanic bigotry, but by 1858 proclamations appointing a day of thanksgiving were issued by the governors of 25 states and two territories.

In the middle of the American Civil War, President Abraham Lincoln, prompted by a series of editorials written by Sarah Josepha Hale, proclaimed a national Thanksgiving Day, to be celebrated on the final Thursday in November 1863:

> "The year that is drawing towards its close, has been filled with the blessings of fruitful fields and healthful skies. To these bounties, which are so constantly enjoyed that we are prone to forget the source from which they come, others have been added, which are of so extraordinary a nature, that they cannot fail to penetrate and soften even the heart which is habitually insensible to the ever watchful providence of Almighty God. In the midst of a civil war of unequalled magnitude and severity, which has sometimes seemed to foreign States to invite and to provoke their aggression, peace has been preserved with all nations, order has been maintained, the laws have been respected and obeyed, and harmony has prevailed

Thanksgiving *(con't)*

everywhere except in the theatre of military conflict; while that theatre has been greatly contracted by the advancing armies and navies of the Union. Needful diversions of wealth and of strength from the fields of peaceful industry to the national defence, have not arrested the plough, the shuttle, or the ship; the axe had enlarged the borders of our settlements, and the mines, as well of iron and coal as of the precious metals, have yielded even more abundantly than heretofore. Population has steadily increased, notwithstanding the waste that has been made in the camp, the siege and the battle-field; and the country, rejoicing in the consciousness of augmented strength and vigor, is permitted to expect continuance of years, with large increase of freedom.

No human counsel hath devised nor hath any mortal hand worked out these great things. They are the gracious gifts of the Most High God, who, while dealing with us in anger for our sins, hath nevertheless remembered mercy.

It has seemed to me fit and proper that they should be solemnly, reverently and gratefully acknowledged as with one heart and voice by the whole American people. I do therefore invite my fellow citizens in every part of the United States, and also those who are at sea and those who are sojourning in foreign lands, to set apart and observe the last Thursday of November next, as a day of Thanksgiving and Praise to our beneficent Father who dwelleth in the Heavens. And I recommend to them that while offering up the ascriptions justly due to Him for such singular deliverances and blessings,

Thanksgiving *(con't)*

they do also, with humble penitence for our national perverseness and disobedience, commend to his tender care all those who have become widows, orphans, mourners or sufferers in the lamentable civil strife in which we are unavoidably engaged, and fervently implore the interposition of the Almighty Hand to heal the wounds of the nation and to restore it as soon as may be consistent with the Divine purposes to the full enjoyment of peace, harmony, tranquility and Union.

In testimony whereof, I have hereunto set my hand, and caused the seal of the United States to be affixed.

Done at the city of Washington, this third day of October, in the year of our Lord one thousand eight hundred and sixty-three, and of the independence of the United States the eighty-eighth.
Proclamation of President Abraham Lincoln, 3 October 1863."

Since 1863, Thanksgiving has been observed annually in the United States.] {20}

Don't tell us this nation wasn't founded on Biblical morals and principles!

[Thanksgiving is a national harvest holiday celebrated primarily in North America. In Canada, Thanksgiving Day is celebrated on the second Monday in October. In the United States, it is celebrated on the last Thursday in November and commemorates a meal shared between colonists and Native Americans in 1621.

Thanksgiving (con't)

Although it is rooted in the history of the Pilgrims (who were Christian "Separatists"), the American Thanksgiving is no longer generally considered a religious holiday, but a day to gather with family, eat an astounding amount of food, watch football and parades, and be thankful for the blessings of life.

The "first Thanksgiving" in 1621 has little in common with the modern-day celebration. It began when some colonists at Plymouth went out "fowling," probably for geese and ducks rather than the harder-to-catch turkeys, since they reported they "in one day killed as much as... served the company almost a week." Other items on the menu probably included fish, eels, shellfish, stews, vegetables, and beer.

After the successful hunt, 90 or so Wampanoag made a surprise appearance at the settlement's gate. Although this may have been initially alarming to the colonists, who numbered about 50, the groups socialized peacefully over the next few days. The Wampanoag contributed venison to the feast and joined the Pilgrims for activities like shooting guns, running races and drinking liquor. The end result of the rather disorderly party was a treaty between the two groups that lasted until King Philip's War in 1675.

The early colonists of New England regularly celebrated "Thanksgivings" after a military victory, end to a drought, or other favorable event. For example, a national Thanksgiving was proclaimed upon the enactment of the Constitution. The Christian group known as the Separatists (later called Pilgrims) generally shunned holidays, but periodically proclaimed a Day of Thanksgiving and Praise in response to evidence of God's favor or a Day of Humiliation and Fasting in response to God's perceived displeasure. These feast and fast days were usually

Thanksgiving (con't)

held on the day of special sermons called "Lecture Day," which was Thursday in Massachusetts.

The first general (not in response to any particular event) day of Thanksgiving was proclaimed by President George Washington, who at the request of Congress recommended Thursday, 26 November, 1789, to the people of the United States "as a day of public thanksgiving and prayer to be observed by acknowledging with grateful hearts the many and signal favours of Almighty God." However, after 1798 the proclamation of a Thanksgiving Day was left to the states, for Southerners were slow to adopt the custom, some objected to the federal government's involvement in religious observance, and others disliked the partisan speeches and parades that became customary.

Thanksgiving Day only became an official holiday once Northerners dominated the federal government. In 1863, after the famous battle at Gettysburg, Abraham Lincoln proclaimed a national day of Thanksgiving to be held on August 6. Soon the public began to ask for an annual observance, so in 1867, President Andrew Johnson established the last Thursday in November as the official Thanksgiving Day. Two attempts were made by later presidents to adjust the date: in 1870 Ulysses S. Grant moved it to November 18 and from 1939 to 1941, Franklin D. Roosevelt moved it back a week to extend the Christmas shopping season.

The tradition of Thanksgiving football games began with a game between Yale and Princeton in 1876. In the late 1800s, parades of costumed revelers became common, and in 1924 the first annual Macy's parade was conducted. Giant balloons were added in 1927 and have been a staple ever since.

Thanksgiving (con't)

In Canada, Thanksgiving Days also arose during the colonial period. The earliest Canadian Thanksgiving was held in 1578, when Martin Frobisher held a ceremony in present-day Newfoundland to give thanks for a safe arrival in the New World. In 1879, Parliament established a national Thanksgiving day on November 6; since 1957, Thanksgiving Day has been celebrated in Canada on the second Monday in October.

Today, Thanksgiving is a time when families who live far apart gather together to feast on turkey and trimmings, watch or play football, and enjoy parades. Its meaning has also changed over the years: "The holiday associated with Pilgrims and Native Americans has come to symbolize intercultural peace, America's opportunity for newcomers, and the sanctity of home and family."

In the United States, Thanksgiving is an official holiday on which all public business is suspended. It has become traditional for the President to pardon a lucky turkey from gracing anyone's dinner table on Thanksgiving Day. On a recent Thanksgiving, after pardoning "Liberty," the freed bird, President Bush *(George W.)* said, "Through the generations, our country has known its share of hardships. ... Yet, we've never lost sight of the blessings around us: the freedoms we enjoy, the people we love, and the many gifts of our prosperous land."

The Friday after Thanksgiving has become the unofficial start to the Christmas season. Many stores host sales on this day to encourage shoppers to begin their Christmas shopping, so it is also the day to either flock to the malls or avoid the malls completely, depending on one's temperament.] {33}

St Andrew's Day

Origin Date: appr 4th Century
Originator(s): Constantine (beginnings of Catholicism)
Man's Description: [St. Andrew's Day is celebrated on November 30, and honors Andrew, the brother of St. Peter and patron saint of Scotland and Russia. Today, it plays a similar role as St Patrick's Day for Ireland — it is a day for celebrating Scottish culture.

Saint Andrew was the brother of Saint Peter and is regarded as the first of the twelve apostles. Like Peter, Andrew was a fisherman from Bethsaida in Galilee. Andrew was a disciple of John the Baptist who had followed Jesus on John's recommendation. According to a New Testament account:

> Andrew, Simon Peter's brother, was one of the two who heard what John had said and who had followed Jesus. The first Andrew did was to find his brother Simon and tell him, "We have found the Messiah." And he brought him to Jesus. (John 1:40-42)

According to tradition, St. Andrew conducted missionary work around the Black Sea. Early apocryphal accounts describing Andrew's life include the *Acts of Andrew, Acts of Andrew and Matthias,* and *Acts of Peter and Andrew.* According to the *Acts of Andrew*, parts of which are now lost, he was martyred by crucifixion in Patras, Achaia (Greece). His death is generally dated to 60, or perhaps 70, AD. No earlier than the 10th century, St. Andrew's cross came to be described as X-shaped. Both Catholic and Orthodox churches recognize St. Andrew's feast day (the traditional day of his martyrdom) on November 30.

St Andrew's Day (con't)

Like most important saints, Andrew was not left in his tomb to rest in peace. According to St. Jerome, Andrew's remains were taken from Patras to Constantinople in the fourth century by order of the Roman emperor Constantine and, according to tradition, a few body parts were taken by St. Rule to Scotland before they made it to Constantinople. These relics were held in St. Andrew's Cathedral, but were likely destroyed in the Scottish Reformation. In 1208, St. Andrew's remains were moved from Constantinople to the Church of Sant' Andrea in Amalfi, Italy. In the 15th century, Andrew's head was brought to St. Peter's Basilica in the Vatican.

In 1879, the Archbishop of Amalfi sent Andrew's shoulder blade to the reestablished Catholic community in Scotland. In September 1964, Pope Paul VI returned Andrew's head to Patras as a gesture of goodwill to the Christians in Greece. In 1969, when Gordon Gray was in Rome to be appointed the first Scottish Cardinal since the Reformation, he was given some relics of St. Andrew with the words, "Saint Peter gives you his brother." These are now displayed in a reliquary in St. Mary's Roman Catholic Cathedral in Edinburgh.

Saint Andrew is the patron saint of Russia and Scotland, as well as fishermen, singers, unmarried women, and would-be mothers.

There are a variety of explanations as to how St. Andrew came to be associated with Scotland. According to the most traditional tale, when Constantine ordered Andrew's relics to be moved to Constantinople, an angel appeared to St. Rule (or Regulus) in a dream and told him to take some of the relics to the ends of the earth for safekeeping. He obediently took a tooth, an arm bone, a kneecap and some fingers from Andrew's

St Andrew's Day (con't)

tomb and sailed north with the remains until he was shipwrecked on the east coast of Scotland. There he established the city of St. Andrew's, and the relics were placed in a specially constructed chapel.

In 1160, the chapel was replaced by St. Andrew's Cathedral, which became an important medieval pilgrimmage destination. Much of the cathedral is in ruins today, but "St. Rule's Tower" is one of the buildings that remains. As noted above, St. Andrew's relics were probably destroyed during the Scottish Reformation, but a plaque among the ruins of the cathedral shows modern visitors where the relics were kept.

One of the earliest times St. Andrew was recognized as the patron saint of Scotland was at the signing of the Declaration of Arbroath in 1320. Signed by Robert the Bruce and other Scottish noblemen, the Declaration asserted Scotland's independence from England.

According to legend, however, St. Andrew became the patron saint of Scotland much earlier, in 832 AD. In a story that resembles the famous tale of Emperor Constantine and the Chi Rho, it is said that an army of Scots was facing an English army when the Scottish king prayed to St. Andrew for help. Seeing a cloud in the shape of the saltire (X-shaped) cross against a clear blue sky, the king vowed that if the Scots were victorious, St. Andrew would be made the patron saint of Scotland. The Scots won the battle, the king fulfilled his promise, and the intervention of St. Andrew has been represented on the Scottish flag ever since.

St. Andrew's Day is celebrated on November 30th each year, the traditional date of St. Andrew's martyrdom in Greece. The

St Andrew's Day (con't)

holiday is important for all liturgical Christians, as the beginning of Advent is set at the Sunday closest to St. Andrew's Day.

Among Scots, especially those who are away from their homeland, November 30 is a day for celebrating the best of Scottish culture and cuisine. As one would expect, the focal point of St. Andrew's Day in Scotland is the city of St. Andrew's in Fife, which is about an hour north of Edinburgh. There, throughout "St. Andrew's Week," one can attend traditional music concerts, special church services, porridge-making contests, piping contests and ceilidhs, watch fireworks, and visit places that are not normally open to the public, like the Masonic Lodge and the private areas of the famous Royal and Ancient Golf Course. Elsewhere in Scotland, many schools hold a special assembly focusing on the patron saint and Scotland, special events are held at landmarks like the Edinburgh Castle, and friends gather for ceilidhs, haggis suppers, general whisky drinking, or other celebrations of Scottish heritage.

However, the popularity of St. Andrew's Day in Scotland is a relatively recent and still-growing development. This is only the ninth year of St. Andrew's Week, and November 30 is not a national holiday. In 2001, Scotch whisky manufacturer Famous Grouse conducted a survey throughout Scotland that showed only 22 percent of Scots knew when St. Andrew's Day is celebrated.] {34}

Christmas

Origin Date: appr 336 AD; declared a US federal holiday June 26, 1870
Originator(s): Constantine (beginnings of Catholicism)
Man's Description: [The celebration of the birth of Jesus Christ that is observed on December 25th.

The English word "Christmas" derives from the old English Christes maesse, meaning "Christ's mass." Unlike Easter, **Christmas was not celebrated by the earliest Christians**. It began to be observed in the late 3rd century AD as an alternative to pagan winter holidays.

Christians have been celebrating Jesus' birth on December 25th since at least the early fourth century. The first evidence of its observance is in Rome in 336 AD. The earliest Christians do not appear to have commemorated the nativity, but only the baptism and resurrection of Christ and the deaths of the martyrs.

In fact, some early Christians, most notably Origen of Alexandria strongly opposed the celebration of Christ's birth. Point out that only Pharoah and Herod celebrate their birthdays in the Bible. Origen argued that birthdays were for pagans, not Christians. Jehovah's Witnesses follow this line of reasoning today in rejecting both Christmas and celebration of birthdays.] {35}

[The Romans held a festival on December 25 called *Dies Natalis Solis Invicti,* "the birthday of the undefeated sun." The use of the title Sol Invictus allowed several solar deities to be worshipped collectively, including Elah-Gabal, a Syrian sun god; Sol, the god of Emperor Aurelian (AD 270–274); and Mithras, a soldiers' god of Persian origin. Emperor Elagabalus

Christmas (con't)

(218–222) introduced the festival, and it reached the height of its popularity under Aurelian, who promoted it as an empire-wide holiday.

December 25 was also considered to be the date of the winter solstice, which the Romans called *bruma.* It was therefore the day the Sun proved itself to be "unconquered" despite the shortening of daylight hours. (When Julius Caesar introduced the Julian Calendar in 45 BC, December 25 was approximately the date of the solstice. In modern times, the solstice falls on December 21 or 22.) The Sol Invictus festival has a "strong claim on the responsibility" for the date of Christmas, according to the *Catholic Encyclopedia.* Several early Christian writers connected the rebirth of the sun to the birth of Jesus "O, how wonderfully acted Providence that on that day on which that Sun was born . . . Christ should be born", Cyrian wrote.

Pagan Scandinavia celebrated a winter festival called Yule, held in the late December to early January period. Yule logs were lit to honor Thor, the god of thunder, with the belief that each spark from the fire represented a new pig or calf that would be born during the coming year. Feasting would continue until the log burned out, which could take as many as twelve days. In pagan Germania (not to be confused with Germany), the equivalent holiday was the mid-winter night which was followed by 12 "*wild nights*", filled with eating, drinking and partying. As Northern Europe was the last part to Christianize, its pagan celebrations had a major influence on Christmas. Scandinavians still call Christmas *Jul.* In English, the Germanic word Yule is synonymous with Christmas, a usage first recorded in 900.

Christmas (con't)

It is unknown exactly when or why December 25 became associated with Christ's birth. The New Testament does not give a specific date. Sextus Julius Africanus popularized the idea that Christ was born on December 25 in his *Chronographiai*, a reference book for Christians written in AD 221.

The Christmas tree is often explained as a Christianization of pagan tradition and ritual surrounding the Winter Solstice, which included the use of evergreen boughs, and an adaptation of pagan tree worship.] {21}

Was Yeshua really born around December 25th? Let us look at scripture:

(1) And it came to pass in those days, that there went out a
decree from Caesar Augustus, that all the world should be
taxed. (2) (*And* this taxing was first made when Cyrenius
was governor of Syria.) (3) And all went to be taxed, every
one into his own city. (4) And Joseph also went up from
Galilee, out of the city of Nazareth, into Judaea, unto the
city of David, which is called Bethlehem; (because he was
of the house and lineage of David:) (5) To be taxed with
Mary his espoused wife, being great with child. (6) And so
it was, that, while they were there, the days were
accomplished that she should be delivered. (7) And she
brought forth her firstborn son, and wrapped him in
swaddling clothes, and laid him in a manger; because there
was no room for them in the inn. (8) And there were in
the same country shepherds abiding in the field, keeping
watch over their flock by night. (9) And, lo, the angel of

Christmas (con't)

the Lord came upon them, and the glory of the Lord shone
round about them: and they were sore afraid. **(10)** And
the angel said unto them, Fear not: for, behold, I bring you
good tidings of great joy, which shall be to all people. **(11)**
For unto you is born this day in the city of David a Saviour,
which is Christ the Lord. **(12)** And this *shall be* a sign unto
you; Ye shall find the babe wrapped in swaddling clothes,
lying in a manger. **(13)** And suddenly there was with the
angel a multitude of the heavenly host praising God, and
saying, **(14)** Glory to God in the highest, and on earth
peace, good will toward men. **(15)** And it came to pass, as
the angels were gone away from them into heaven, the
shepherds said one to another, Let us now go even unto
Bethlehem, and see this thing which is come to pass, which
the Lord hath made known unto us. **(16)** And they came
with haste, and found Mary, and Joseph, and the babe
lying in a manger.

---Luke 2:1-16 (KJV)

In verse 8 above the shepherds were tending their flocks at night. This indicates that this was a warmer season instead of winter. Tending of the flocks during winter was primarily done during the day. The development of Christmas has it's roots from Constantine who was a sun worshipper who invented the Christmas celebration in hopes of combining Christian beliefs and desire to acknowledge Yeshua's birth along with the pagan celebration of Nimrod's birthday which is on December 25th.

Christmas (con't)

It is believed by many who study the Festivals and our Hebraic roots that Yeshua was born during the Feast of Tabernacles also know as the Feast of Ingathering.

> **(14)** And the Word became flesh, and dwelt among us (and we beheld his glory, glory as of the only begotten from the Father), full of grace and truth.
>
> **---John 1:14 (ASV)**

[Many scholars believe Yeshua was born on the first day of Sukkot (Feast of Tabernacles) and circumcised on the eighth day of Shemini Atzeret.

The birth of Yeshua occurred six months after the birth of John the Baptist. The Book of Luke tells the story (Luke 1:5-80). Knowing when the priest Zechariah burned incense in the Temple tells us when his son, John the Baptist, was born. Six months after John was born, Mary gave birth to Yeshua in Bethlehem.

Zechariah served with the priestly division of Abijah. King David had divided all priests into 24 divisions around 1000 B.C.E. Abijah was the eighth division. He gave them job descriptions and a schedule of Temple service (1 Chronicles 24).

Each division served for seven days, beginning and ending on a Sabbath (1 Chronicles 9:25-26 and 2 Chronicles 23:4-8). When they arrived in Jerusalem, they cast lots to determine specific tasks.

Christmas (con't)

Rabbis say the 24 divisions served a week during the first half of the year, and a week during the second half, totaling 48 weeks of service. In addition, they all served for three pilgrimage feasts. The 51 weeks of service was a full Jewish year.

The religious year began in Nisan, between mid-March and mid-April. Two weeks after the year started, all 24 divisions reported to Jerusalem for the first pilgrimage feast, the Feast of Unleavened Bread. Seven weeks later, they all returned for the second pilgrimage feast, the Feast of Weeks. As the eighth division, the Abijah division would not have served until the tenth week of the year Zechariah, along with the entire Abijah division, was in Jerusalem between the second and third Sabbaths of Sivan, around Sivan 12-18.

As Zechariah burned incense, an angel appeared and told him his wife Elizabeth would give birth to a son named John. Elizabeth became pregnant when Zechariah returned home, after the third week of Sivan, in mid-June (Luke 1:23-24).

Allowing forty weeks for a normal pregnancy, John the Baptist was born the following Passover. Interestingly, one Passover custom is to set a special place at the table for Elijah, because Elijah returns before Messiah comes (Malachi 4:5). Yeshua said that John was the Elijah who was to come (Matthew 11:13:15)! Even the angel said that Elijah's spirit would rest on John the Baptist (Luke 1:17).

Exactly six months after Elizabeth became pregnant, the angel Gabriel appeared to Mary (Luke 1:26-33). It was the month of Kislev (December). He said she would bear the Messiah and

Christmas (con't)

her elderly relative Elizabeth was already six months pregnant. After the angel's visit, Mary supernaturally conceived Yeshua.

Elizabeth became pregnant with John the Baptist in the third week of Sivan (June). Mary became pregnant with Yeshua six months later, in the third week of Kislev. Since Hanukkah begins on Kislev 25, Yeshua, the Light of the World, was conceived during the Festival of Lights!

John was born during Passover in the middle of Nisan, the first month. Yeshua was born six months later during Sukkot in the middle of Tishri (Sept.), the seventh month. "The Word became flesh and tabernacled among us" (John 1:14)!

Near Messiah's birth, Mary and Joseph returned to Bethlehem to register in a Roman census. Romans scheduled the census after the fall harvest to tax the crops. With no room at the inn, they were offered a sukkah erected for Sukkot.

Sukkot is the time when shepherds watched their flocks by night, as they did when Yeshua was born. During winter, lambs stayed indoors. The major theme of Sukkot is joy and angels used this word when they announced his birth (Luke 2:10).

In ancient times, a pagan mass for the Babylonian prince Tammuz was Thebeth 25 or December 25. Rome renamed it Christ's Mass or Christmas.] {11}

It is also interesting that the sign (constellation) of the "virgin", Virgo, is well known during the Feast of Tabernacles. Could this be the "sign" described in Revelation 12?

Christmas (con't)

> **(1)** And a great sign was seen in heaven: a woman arrayed with the sun, and the moon under her feet, and upon her head a crown of twelve stars; **(2)** and she was with child; and she crieth out, travailing in birth, and in pain to be delivered.
>
> **---Revelation 12:1-2 (ASV)**

[The constellation known to us today as Virgo depicts a woman, and the sun passes through this constellation during mid-September.] {12} This is during the same season as The Feast of Tabernacles.

> **(2)** This is what the LORD says: "Don't learn the way of the nations, and don't be terrified by signs in the heavens, though the nations are terrified of them.
>
> **---Jeremiah 10:2 (ISV)**

Holiday Observations

In researching the history of the previously mentioned Christian holidays, we have come to the following conclusions with which we think you will agree after reading the material:

1.) Most holidays we currently observe originated from Catholicism and/or were derived from pagan-related festivals or celebrations originally honoring a pagan deity (god):
    - a.) Sunday – instituted by Catholicism with pagan-related festivities incorporated
    - b.) Epiphany – instituted as holiday by Catholicism
    - c.) Mardi Gras – instituted as holiday by Catholicism
    - d.) Ash Wednesday – instituted as holiday by Catholicism
    - e.) Lent – instituted as holiday by Catholicism
    - f.) Valentine's Day – pagan-related origins
    - g.) Palm Sunday – instituted as holiday by Catholicism
    - h.) St. Patrick's Day – instituted as holiday by Catholicism, honoring Saint Patrick
    - i.) Good Friday – instituted as holiday by Catholicism
    - j.) Easter – instituted as holiday by Catholicism, pagan-related festivities incorporated
    - k.) Halloween – pagan-related festivities, Celtic origin
    - l.) Thanksgiving – feast of Thanksgiving honoring the Heavenly Father (YHWH); reminds us of the Holy Day of Feast of Tabernacles which is thanksgiving for the fruit harvest

Holiday Observations *(con't)*

m.) St. Andrew's Day – instituted as holiday by Catholicism, honoring Saint Andrew brother of Saint Peter

n.) Christimas – instituted as holiday by Catholicism, pagan-related festivities incorporated. *We found it interesting that it was not declared a US holiday until 1870*

2.) All are MAN created with only a few stemming from scriptural reference but were not declared as Holy Days in scripture. MAN declared them, not YHWH.

3.) There is diversity (lack of unity) in the days of celebration and ways of celebration of the majority of holidays. Their days of observance seem to be regulated by geographical location of observers and by denominational doctrine or dogma. Man has adjusted the "times" of these celebrations throughout their existence based on what sometimes seems man's "whim" or ideology/theology of a given time in history.

4.) We found it ironic that people of ANY nationality or faith can observe these man-created holidays while many people believe they must be of Jewish or Israeli descent to honor the festivals, Holy Days, given to us by YHWH Himself.

Holiday Observations *(con't)*

Scripture tells us ***not to do what is right in our own eyes but do what is right in the eyes of YHWH:***

> **(7)** The Law of the LORD is perfect, restoring life. The testimony of the LORD is steadfast, making foolish people wise. **(8)** The precepts of the LORD are upright, making the heart rejoice. The commandment of the LORD is pure, giving light to the eyes.
>
> **---Psalm 19:7-8 (ISV)**

> **(15)** The way of a fool is right in his own eyes; But he that is wise hearkeneth unto counsel.
>
> **---Proverbs 12:15 (ASV)**

> **(2)** Every man's lifestyle is proper in his own view, but the LORD weighs the heart.
>
> **---Proverbs 21:2 (ISV)**

> **(4)** Ye shall not do so unto the LORD your God. **(5)** But unto the place which the LORD your God shall choose out of all your tribes to put his name there, *even* unto his habitation shall ye seek, and thither thou shalt come: **(6)** And thither ye shall bring your burnt offerings, and your sacrifices, and your tithes, and heave offerings of your hand, and your vows, and your freewill offerings, and the firstlings of your herds and of your flocks: **(7)** And there ye shall eat before the LORD your God, and ye shall rejoice in all that ye put your hand unto, ye and your households, wherein the

Holiday Observations (con't)

> LORD thy God hath blessed thee. **(8)** Ye shall not do after all *the things* that we do here this day, every man whatsoever *is* right in his own eyes.
>
> **---Deuteronomy 12:4-8 (KJV)**

> **(17)** Moreover, you must never take any item from those condemned things, so the LORD may yet relent from his burning anger and extend compassion, have mercy, and cause you to increase in number—as he promised by an oath to your ancestors— **(18)** if you obey the voice of the LORD your God by observing all his commands that I'm commanding you today. Do what is right in the sight of the LORD your God."
>
> **---Deuteronomy 13:17-18 (ISV)**

The following scripture was sobering to us and made us stop and ask if we have inherited lies and things of vanity. It is our firm belief, YES, we have!

> **(19)** O LORD, my strength, and my fortress, and my refuge in the day of affliction, the Gentiles shall come unto thee from the ends of the earth, and shall say, Surely our fathers have inherited lies, vanity, and *things* wherein *there is* no profit.
>
> **---Jeremiah 16:19 (KJV)**

History, Origins & Description of YHWH's Holy Days

And the LORD spake unto Moses, saying, speak unto the children of Israel, and say unto them, *Concerning* the feasts of the LORD, which ye shall proclaim *to be* holy convocations, *even* these *are* my feasts.
---Leviticus 23:1 & 2 (KJV)

Holy Convocations are defined as the following by Strong's Concordance via e-sword:

H6944 קֹדֶשׁ

qôdesh *ko'-desh*

From H6942; a *sacred* place or thing; rarely abstractly *sanctity:* - consecrated (thing), dedicated (thing), hallowed (thing), holiness, (X most) holy (X day, portion, thing), saint, sanctuary.

H4744 מִקְרָא

miqrâ' *mik-raw'*

From H7121; something *called* out, that is, a public *meeting* (the act, the persons, or the place); also a *rehearsal:* - assembly, calling, convocation, reading. {1}

Holy Days – Sabbath (Shabbat)			
Day(s) of Observance	Weekly Sabbath - each seventh day (Saturday). The weekly Sabbath is scripturally said to be a sign and perpetual covenant between YHWH and His family of believers forever. The Sabbath applies to not only the House of Israel, but also to the stranger that has joined himself to the Lord. Various festivals also have Sabbath Days of Rest (see below).		
Observed By & For How Long	House of Israel and stranger that has joined himself to the Lord. Sign & perpetual covenant forever		
Sabbath Days of Rest	Weekly; no work of any kind for you or your children, servants, work animals or stranger who stays with you (Exo. 20:10)	Fast Day(s)	No
Scriptural Observance	►rest from work ►do not kindle fire ►no selling of provisions ►carry no burden out of your houses ►keep it holy (set-apart) ►do not pollute the Sabbath (pollute=wound, dissolve, profane) ►burnt offering: two blemishless lambs ►meal/grain (fine flour mingled with oil) offering by fire ►drink offering		
Man's Traditional Observance	Many observances are reminiscent of Pharisaical law. Some go so far as to say you cannot turn a light switch on during the Sabbath. This is NOT scriptural! Yeshua was rebuked by the Pharisees for healing on the Sabbath. His response was that it is good to do good on the Sabbath.		
Did Yeshua Observe?	Yes. As the spotless lamb of YHWH, he was a Torah observant Jew. He declared Himself Lord of the Sabbath in the Renewed Covenant.		

Holy Days - Passover (Pesach)			
Day(s) of Observance	14th day of the first month (Nisan or Aviv=March or April timeframe) .		
Observed By & For How Long	Pilgrimage feast. All Hebrew males of the House of Israel and stranger that has joined himself to the Lord are required to make pilgrimage to Jerusalem. No stranger, foreigner or hired servant. No one uncircumcised. "There shall no stranger eat thereof: But every man's servant that is bought for money, when thou hast circumcised him, then shall he eat thereof. A foreigner and a hired servant shall not eat thereof." Are we not purchased by Yeshua's blood? "And this day shall be unto you for a memorial; and ye shall keep it a feast to the LORD throughout your generations; ye shall keep it a feast by an ordinance forever."		
Sabbath Days of Rest	No	Fast Day(s)	No
Scriptural Observance	▶memorial ▶unleavened bread ▶bitter herbs ▶slaughtering of lamb, roasted over fire ▶if any remains overnight, burn with fire ▶eaten in one house ▶eat with loins girded, shoes on, staff in hand		
Man's Traditional Observance	▶spring cleaning (removing all leaven) ▶Fast of the Firstborn Nisan 13 (firstborn males) ▶hametz-children's game: searching for bread crumbs night before ▶candle lighting Passover Seders are held by many believers today. Traditions for the meal include: ▶blessings ▶4 cups wine ▶bitter herbs ▶lamb ▶unleavened bread ▶parsley ▶salt water ▶charoset (mixture of apples, nuts & cinnamon, ▶setting place at table for Elijah		
Did Yeshua Observe?	Yes. Matthew 26:1-5; Matthew 27:15; Mark 14:1-2; Mark 14:12-16; Mark 15:6; Luke 2:41-43; Luke 22:1-13; Luke 23:17; John 2:23; John 4:45; John 6:3-5; John 13:1; John 13:29		

Holy Days - Feast of Unleavened Bread			
Day(s) of Observance	15th day of the first month (Nisan or Aviv= March or April timeframe) for seven days.		
Observed By & For How Long	All the congregation of Israel. No stranger, foreigner or hired servant. No one uncircumcised. "There shall no stranger eat thereof: But every man's servant that is bought for money, when thou hast circumcised him, then shall he eat thereof. A foreigner and an hired servant shall not eat thereof." Are we not purchased by Yeshua's blood? "And this day shall be unto you for a memorial; and ye shall keep it a feast to the LORD throughout your generations; ye shall keep it a feast by an ordinance for ever. "		
Sabbath Days of Rest	1st & 7th days; only work allowed in order to eat	*Fast Day(s)*	No
Scriptural Observance	►no leavening found in dwellings ►eat only unleavened bread		
Man's Traditional Observance	►spring cleaning (removing all leaven) ►avoid eating leavening of any kind for seven days		
Did Yeshua Observe?	Yes. Matthew 26:17; Mark 14:1-2; Mark 14:12-16; Luke 22:1-13		

Holy Days - Day of Firstfruits (Yom HaBikkurim)			
Day(s) of Observance	The day after the first Sabbath of the harvest. This is usually after the barley harvest. Today it is celebrated on Nisan 16th.		
Observed By & For How Long	House of Israel and stranger that has joined himself to the Lord. "It shall be a statute forever throughout your generations in all your dwellings."		
Sabbath Days of Rest	No	Fast Day(s)	No
Scriptural Observance	▶wave offering by Priest on day after the Sabbath of the harvest ▶burnt offering: blemish less he lamb ▶meal/grain (fine flour mingled with oil) offering by fire ▶wine offering ▶cannot eat of the harvest until first fruit offerings are made		
Man's Traditional Observance	▶special meal, no leaven ▶scripture readings ▶blessings		
Did Yeshua Observe?	Yes. As the spotless lamb of YHWH, he was a Torah observant Jew. He and the Father are one and the same.		

Holy Days - Feast of Weeks (Pentecost)			
Day(s) of Observance	Fifty days after the feast of Firstfruits.		
Observed By & For How Long	Pilgrimage feast. All Hebrew males of the House of Israel and stranger that has joined himself to the Lord are required to make pilgrimage to Jerusalem. Festive meal consisting of offerings to be shared with rejoicing among family members, Levites, strangers, fatherless & widows at Jerusalem. "It shall be a statute for ever in all your dwellings throughout your generations."		
Sabbath Days of Rest	Yes, no servile work	*Fast Day(s)*	No
Scriptural Observance	►first fruits of harvest placed in basket and brought to place that YHWH has put His name upon ►speak before YHWH at time of offering ►wave offering: two leavened loaves ►burnt offerings: seven lambs without blemish of the first year, one young bullock, & two rams ►sin offering: one kid goat ►peace offering: two lambs of the first year ►meal/grain & drink offerings		
Man's Traditional Observance	►candle lighting ►festive meal, dairy foods & sweet dairy deserts ►challah bread (reminds of bread offering in Temple) ►read book of Ruth & other scriptures ►stay up all night ►plant a tree		
Did Yeshua Observe?	Yes. As the spotless lamb of YHWH, he was a Torah observant Jew. He and the Father are one and the same.		

Holy Days – Day of Trumpets (Yom Teruah)			
Day(s) of Observance	1st day of the seventh month (Tishri=September or October depending on the new moon sighting).		
Observed By & For How Long	House of Israel and stranger that has joined himself to the Lord.		
Sabbath Days of Rest	Yes, no servile work	Fast Day(s)	No
Scriptural Observance	▶memorial of blowing trumpets ▶burnt offering: one young bullock, one ram, & seven lambs of the first year without blemish ▶meal/grain (fine flour mingled with oil) offering by fire ▶sin offering: one kid goat ▶drink offering		
Man's Traditional Observance	▶festive meal, apple slices dipped in honey ▶blessings ▶blowing of shofar ▶read scriptures		
Did Yeshua Observe?	Yes. As the spotless lamb of YHWH, he was a Torah observant Jew. He and the Father are one and the same.		

Note: Rosh HaShanah is observed during this timeframe. Rosh HaShanah means "head of the year". It is a festival of the people, and is not a holy day declared by YHWH in scripture.

Holy Days - Day of Atonement (Yom Kippur) (The Great Day)			
Day(s) of Observance	10th day of the seventh month (Tishri=September or October depending on the new moon sighting). **Note**: *Scripture tells us that the "fast" begins at the evening of the 9th day and ends at the evening of the 10th day.*		
Observed By & For How Long	House of Israel and stranger that has joined himself to the Lord. "It shall be a statute forever throughout your generations in all your dwellings."		
Sabbath Days of Rest	Yes, no work of any kind	*Fast Day(s)*	Yes
Scriptural Observance	▶burnt offering: one young bullock, one ram, & seven lambs of the first year without blemish ▶meal/grain (fine flour mingled with oil) offering by fire ▶sin offering: one kid goat ▶drink offering		
Man's Traditional Observance	▶repentance ▶fasting ▶read scriptures		
Did Yeshua Observe?	Yes. As the spotless lamb of YHWH, he was a Torah observant Jew. He and the Father are one and the same.		

Holy Days - Feast of Tabernacles (Sukkot) (Feast of Booths)			
Day(s) of Observance	15th day of the seventh month (Tishri=September or October depending on the new moon sighting) lasting for eight days.		
Observed By & For How Long	Pilgrimage feast. All Hebrew males of the House of Israel and stranger that has joined himself to the Lord are required to make pilgrimage to Jerusalem. Festive meal consisting of offerings to be shared with rejoicing among family members, Levites, strangers, fatherless & widows at Jerusalem. "It shall be a statute for ever in your generations: ye shall celebrate it in the seventh month."		
Sabbath Days of Rest	1st & 8th days, no servile work	Fast Day(s)	No
Scriptural Observance	►rejoice for seven days before YHWH with boughs of goodly trees, branches of palm trees, the boughs of thick trees, & willows of the brook ►dwell in booths seven days; all that are Israelites born shall dwell in booths		
Man's Traditional Observance	►assemble citron fruit (etrog) & branches of myrtle, willow, & palm (lulav) ►build a temporary booth (sukkah) to dine & sleep in ►read scriptures ►blessings		
Did Yeshua Observe?	Yes. John 7:1-26; John 7:37-38; John 12:12-13		

Feast of Dedication (Hanukkah) (Festival of Lights)			
Day(s) of Observance	25th of Kislev (December) lasting eight days. Note: 25th of Kislev is determined by the sighting of the new moon. Not to be confused with Christmas.		
Observed By & For How Long	Festival of the people. Observed by the house of Israel and stranger that has joined himself to the Lord. Refer to book of Maccabees for full detail.		
Sabbath Days of Rest	No	*Fast Day(s)*	No
Scriptural Observance	►none given in scripture		
Man's Traditional Observance	►driedel game for children ►foods cooked in oil ►lighting of hanukkiah ►reading blessings & scriptures dealing with "light"		
Did Yeshua Observe?	Unclear. John 10:22-23 states that Yeshua walked in the temple in Solomon's porch during this feast. It does not state as to whether He participated in observance or not.		

Sabbath

Genesis 2:3 (KJV) And God blessed the seventh day, and sanctified it: because that in it he had rested from all his work which God created and made.

Origin Date: ***7th Day of Creation***
Originator(s): YHWH (God of Israel)
Description: Weekly day of rest as designated by YHWH (there are also "high" Sabbaths related to some of the festivals).

The Hebrew word "Shabbat" means "to cease".
Sabbath came before God gave the commandments on Mount Sinai.

[In Christianity, the **Sabbath** is generally a weekly religious day of rest as ordained by one of the Ten Commandments…. The practice is inherited from Judaism, the parent religion of Christianity; *shabbat* (Hebrew: שַׁבָּת, *šhabbat*) means "the [day of] rest" and entails a ceasing or resting from labor. The institution of the Old Testament Sabbath, taken as a "perpetual covenant ... a sign for ever" by the people of Israel (Exodus 31:16-17-NRSV), was in respect for the day during which God rested after having completed the Creation in six days (Genesis 2:2-3, Exodus 20:8-11).

Originally denoting a rest day on the seventh day of the week (in Judaism, the period from Friday sunset to Saturday nightfall), the term "Sabbath" has acquired the connotation of a time of communal worship and now has several meanings in Christian contexts…

Sabbath *(con't)*

The following are some of the New Testament reasons adduced for keeping the seventh day of the week (Saturday) as a Sabbath day of rest. Sabbatarians take the statement made by Jesus, before the foundation for the Christian Church, that "the Son of Man is lord even of the Sabbath", to indicate that Sabbath-keeping is central to following Christ: since He kept the seventh-day Sabbath, this is the true Lord 's Day. Further, in Matthew 24:20, Christ recommended his listeners, in reference to the future destruction of Jerusalem, "And pray that your flight may not be in winter or on the Sabbath." Sabbath in Christianity / Sabbatarians maintains that this indicates that Jesus expected the Sabbath to be kept after his death. Luke 23:56 recounts that, after the death of Jesus, the women who wished to prepare his body rested on the Sabbath, intending to finish their work on the first day of the week, but on finding he was risen were unable to do so. Also, on the weight of Hebrews 4:8-11, which speaks of a sabbath rest superior to the rest that Joshuah won for the Israelites, Sabbatarians say that the Sabbath remains a Christian Holy Day and that Sabbath-keeping is an abiding duty as prescribed in the fourth commandment.] {22}

Following is material gathered for our personal study on the Sabbath, "*Food for Thought, Sabbath*":
From the beginning YHWH set this special day apart from the rest. He blessed it and sanctified it.

> **(2)** And on the seventh day God ended his work which he had made; and he rested on the seventh day from all his work which he had made. **(3)** And God blessed the seventh day, and sanctified it: because that in it he had rested from all his work which God created and made."
>
> **---Genesis 2:2- 3 (KJV)**

Sabbath (con't)

During their time in the wilderness, YHWH tried to teach the Israelites how special this day is to Him and that it is a "gift" to His people. He also taught that He is our sustenance and that we should be obedient to His Word, not doubting that He will care for us.

> (22) And it came to pass, that on the sixth day they
> gathered twice as much bread, two omers for one man:
> and all the rulers of the congregation came and told
> Moses. (23) And he said unto them, This is that which
> the Lord hath said, tomorrow is the rest of the holy
> Sabbath unto the Lord: bake that which ye will bake
> today, and seethe (boil) that ye will seethe (boil); and
> that which remaineth over lay up for you to be kept
> until the morning. (24) And they laid it up till the
> morning, as Moses bade: and it did not stink, neither
> was there any worm therein. (25) And Moses said, Eat
> that today; for today is a Sabbath unto the Lord: today
> ye shall not find it in the field. (26) Six days ye shall
> gather it; but on the seventh day, which is the Sabbath,
> in it there shall be none. (27) And it came to pass, that
> there went out some of the people on the seventh day
> for to gather, and they found none. (28) And the Lord
> said unto Moses, How long refuse ye to keep my
> commandments and my laws? (29) See, for that the
> Lord hath given you the Sabbath, therefore he giveth
> you on the sixth day the bread of two days; abide ye
> every man in his place, let no man go out of his place
> on the seventh day. (30) So the people rested on the

Sabbath (con't)

> seventh day. **(31)** And the house of Israel called the name thereof Manna: and it was like coriander seed, white; and the taste of it was like wafers made with honey.
>
> **---Exodus 16:22-31 (KJV)**

YHWH's command to keep the Sabbath is also for man's animals, servants, servant's relatives and strangers to rest. It is to be observed even in plowing and harvest time.

> **(12)** Six days thou shalt do thy work, and on the seventh day thou shalt rest; that thine ox and thine ass may have rest, and the son of thy handmaid, and the sojourner, may be refreshed.
>
> **---Exodus 23:12 (ASV)**

> **(21)** "For six days you are to work, but on the seventh day you are to rest; even during plowing time and harvest you are to rest.
>
> **---Exodus 34:21 (ISV)**

Sabbath is an everlasting sign between YHWH and us as the children of Israel forever. It is a perpetual covenant to be observed throughout the generations. YHWH states that the punishment for defiling the Sabbath is death.

> **(12)** And the Lord spake unto Moses, saying, **(13)** Speak thou also unto the children of Israel, saying, Verily my Sabbaths ye shall keep: for it is a sign between me and you throughout your generations; that ye may know that I am the Lord that doth sanctify you.

Sabbath (con't)

> **(14)** Ye shall keep the Sabbath therefore; for it is holy unto you every one that defileth it shall surely be put to death: for whosoever doeth any work therein, that soul shall be cut off from among his people. **(15)** Six days may work be done; but in the seventh is the Sabbath of rest, holy to the Lord: whosoever doeth any work in the Sabbath day, he shall surely be put to death. **(16)** Wherefore the children of Israel shall *keep the Sabbath, to *observe the Sabbath throughout their generations, for a perpetual covenant. **(17)** It is a sign between me and the children of Israel for ever: for in six days the Lord made heaven and earth, and on the seventh day he rested, and was refreshed.
>
> **---Exodus 31:12-17 (KJV)**

> **(1)** And Moses assembled all the congregation of the children of Israel, and said unto them, These are the words which Jehovah hath commanded, that ye should do them. **(2)** Six days shall work be done; but on the seventh day there shall be to you a holy day, a sabbath of solemn rest to Jehovah: whosoever doeth any work therein shall be put to death. **(3)** Ye shall kindle no fire throughout your habitations upon the sabbath day..
>
> **---Exodus 35:1-3 (ASV)**

YHWH upholds His punishment of death for defiling the Sabbath.

> **(32)** And while the children of Israel were in the wilderness, they found a man that gathered sticks upon the

Sabbath (con't)

Sabbath day. **(33)** And they that found him gathering sticks brought him unto Moses and Aaron, and unto all the congregation. **(34)** And they put him in ward (under guard or custody), because it was not declared (explained) what should be done to him. **(35)** And the Lord said unto Moses, The man shall be surely put to death: all the congregation shall stone him with stones without the camp. **(36)** And all the congregation brought him without the camp, and stoned him with stones, and he died; as the Lord commanded Moses.

---Numbers 15:32-36 (KJV)

This shows us how serious YHWH is about observing the Sabbath day and keeping it holy.

More scriptures dealing with the Sabbath:

(3) "Each of you is to fear his mother and father. "Observe my Sabbaths. I am the LORD your God.

---Leviticus 19:3 (ISV)

(30) Ye shall keep (observe) my Sabbaths, and reverence my sanctuary: I am the Lord."

---Leviticus 19:30 (KJV)

(3) Six days you may work, but the seventh day is a Sabbath of rest, a sacred assembly. You are not to do any work. It's a Sabbath to the LORD wherever you live.

---Leviticus 23:3 (ISV)

Sabbath *(con't)*

(1) Thus saith the Lord, Keep ye judgment, and do justice: for my salvation is near to come, and my righteousness to be revealed. **(2)** Blessed is the man that doeth this, and the son of man that layeth hold on it; that keepeth the Sabbath from polluting it, and keepeth his hand from doing any evil. **(3)** Neither let the son of the stranger, that hath joined himself to the Lord, speak, saying, The Lord hath utterly separated me from his people: neither let the eunuch (foreigner) say, Behold, I am a dry tree. **(4)** For thus saith the Lord unto the eunuchs that keep my Sabbaths, and choose the things that please me, and take hold of my covenant; **(5)** Even unto them will I give in mine house and within my walls a place and a name better than of sons and of daughters: I will give them an everlasting name, that shall not be cut off. **(6)** Also the sons of the stranger (foreigner), that join themselves to the Lord, to serve him, and to love the name of the Lord, to be his servants, every one that keepeth the Sabbath from polluting it, and taketh hold of my covenant; **(7)** Even them will I bring to my holy mountain, and make them joyful in my house of prayer: their burnt offerings and their sacrifices shall be accepted upon mine alter; for mine house shall be called a house of prayer for all people.

---Isaiah 56:1-7 (KJV)

Sabbath *(con't)*

> **(13)** "If you keep your feet from trampling the Sabbath, from pursuing your own interests on my holy day, if you call the Sabbath a delight and the LORD's holy day honorable; and if you honor it by not going your own ways and seeking your own pleasure or speaking merely idle words, **(14)** then you will take delight in the LORD, and he will make you ride upon the heights of the earth; and he will make you feast on the inheritance of your ancestor Jacob, your father. "Yes! The mouth of the LORD has spoken."
>
> **---Isaiah 58:13- 14 (ISV)**

Nehemiah, in his position as governor of Judah, tried to correct the defilement of the Sabbath.

> **(15)** In those days saw I in Judah some treading winepresses on the Sabbath, and bringing in sheaves, and lading asses; as also wine, grapes, and figs, and all manner of burdens, which they brought into Jerusalem on the Sabbath day: and I testified against them in the day wherein they sold victuals (provisions). **(16)** There dwelt men of Tyre also therein, which brought fish, and all manner of ware, and sold on the Sabbath unto the children of Judah, and in Jerusalem. **(17)** Then I contended with the nobles of Judah, and said unto them, What evil thing is this that ye do, and profane the Sabbath day? **(18)** Did not your fathers thus, and did not our God bring all this evil (disaster) upon us, and upon this city? Yet ye bring more wrath upon Israel by profaning the Sabbath.

Sabbath (con't)

(19) And it came to pass, that when the gates of Jerusalem began to be dark before the Sabbath, I commanded that the gates should be shut, and charged that they should not be opened till after the Sabbath: and some of my servants set I at the gates, that there should no burden be brought in on the Sabbath day. **(20)** So the merchants and sellers of all kind of ware (merchandise) lodged without Jerusalem once or twice. **(21)** Then I testified against them, and said unto them, Why lodge ye about the wall? If ye do so again, I will lay hands on you. From that time forth came they no more on the Sabbath. **(22)** And I commanded the Levites that they should cleanse themselves, and that they should come and keep the gates, to sanctify the Sabbath day. Remember me, O my God, concerning this also, and spare me according to the greatness of thy mercy.

---Nehemiah 13:15-22 (KJV)

YHWH's judgment upon Judah.

(19) Thus said the Lord unto me; go and stand in the gate of the children of the people, whereby the kings of Judah come in, and by the which they go out, and in all the gates of Jerusalem; **(20)** And say unto them, Hear ye the word of the Lord, ye kings of Judah, and all Judah, and all the inhabitants of Jerusalem, that enter in by these gates: **(21)** Thus saith the Lord; Take heed to yourselves, and bear no burden on the Sabbath day, nor bring it in by the gates of Jerusalem; **(22)** Neither carry forth a burden out of your houses on the Sabbath day, neither do ye any work, but

Sabbath (con't)

hallow ye the Sabbath day, as I commanded your fathers.
(23) But they obeyed not, neither inclined their ear, but made their neck stiff, that they might not hear, nor receive instruction. **(24)** And it shall come to pass, if ye diligently hearken unto me, saith the Lord, to bring in no burden through the gates of this city on the Sabbath day, but hallow the Sabbath day, to do no work therein; **(25)** Then shall there enter into the gates of this city kings and princes sitting upon the throne of David, riding in chariots and on horses, they, and their princes, the men of Judah, and the inhabitants of Jerusalem: and this city shall remain forever. **(26)** And they shall come from the cities of Judah, and from the places about Jerusalem, and from the land of Benjamin, and from the plain, and from the mountains, and from the south, bringing burnt offerings, and sacrifices, and meat offerings, and incense, and bringing sacrifices of praise, unto the house of the Lord. **(27)** But if ye will not hearken unto me to hallow the Sabbath day, and not to bear a burden even entering in at the gates of Jerusalem on the Sabbath day; then will I kindle a fire in the gates thereof, and it shall devour the palaces of Jerusalem, and it shall not be quenched."

---Jeremiah 17:19-27 (KJV)

Millennial Reign (thousand year reign after the Great Tribulation)

(22) For as the new heavens and the new earth, which I will make, shall remain before me, saith the Lord, so shall your seed and your name remain. **(23)** And it shall come

Sabbath *(con't)*

> to pass that from one new moon to another, and from one Sabbath to another, shall all flesh come to worship before me, saith the Lord. **(24)** And they shall go forth, and look upon the carcasses of the men that have transgressed against me: for their worm shall not die, neither shall their fire be quenched; and they shall be an abhorring unto all flesh.
>
> **---Isaiah 66:22-24 (KJV)**

The following scriptures in Ezekiel 20 tell that the children rebelled against YHWH. They did not walk in His statutes, keep His judgments and polluted His Sabbaths. It tells of His mercy once again on a rebellious people. Verses 33-49 prophesy the redemption of the house of Israel. He is now gathering His people once again to redemption. Will we heed the call and return to be His obedient, loving servants doing His will instead of ours?

> **(12)** Moreover also I gave them my Sabbaths, to be a sign between me and them, that they might know that I am the Lord that sanctify them. **(13)** But the house of Israel rebelled against me in the wilderness: they walked not in my statutes, and they despised my judgments, which if a man do, he shall even live in them; and my Sabbaths they greatly polluted: then I said, I would pour out my fury upon them in the wilderness, to consume them. **(14)** But I wrought for my name's sake, that it should not be polluted before the heathen, in whose sight I brought them out. **(15)** Yet also I lifted up my hand unto them in the wilderness, that I would not bring them into the land

Sabbath (con't)

> which I had given them, flowing with milk and honey, which is the glory of all lands; **(16)** because they despised my judgments, and walked not in my statutes, but polluted my Sabbaths: for their heart went after their idols. **(17)** Nevertheless mine eye spared them from destroying them, neither did I make an end of them in the wilderness. **(18)** But I said unto their children in the wilderness, Walk ye not in the statutes of your fathers, neither observe their judgments, nor defile yourselves with their idols: **(19)** I am the Lord your God; walk in my statutes, and keep my judgments, and do them; **(20)** And hallow my Sabbaths; and they shall be a sign between me and you, that ye may know that I am the Lord your God.
>
> **---Ezekiel 20:12-20 (KJV)**

Ezekiel speaks of the coming priesthood that YHWH will restore during the Millennial Reign of Jesus (Yeshua) our Lord and Savior. We will keep YHWH's laws and statutes in His assemblies. We will hallow His Sabbaths.

> **(23)** And they shall teach my people the difference between the holy and the common, and cause them to discern between the unclean and the clean. **(24)** And in a controversy they shall stand to judge; according to mine ordinances shall they judge it: and they shall keep my laws and my statutes in all my appointed feasts; and they shall hallow my sabbaths..
>
> **---Ezekiel 44:23-24 (ASV)**

Sabbath (con't)

Ezekiel also speaks of the prince who will reign during the Millennial Reign. Some believe that the prince mentioned in the prophecy of Ezekiel is David.

> **(4)** For the children of Israel shall abide many days without a king, and without a prince, and without a sacrifice, and without an image, and without an ephod, and without teraphim (*household idol*). **(5)** Afterward shall the children of Israel return, and seek the Lord their God, and David their king; and shall fear the Lord and his goodness in the latter days.
>
> **---Hosea 3:4-5 (KJV)**

> **(23)** "'Then I'll install one shepherd for them—my servant David—and he will feed them, will be there for them, and will serve as their shepherd. **(24)** I, the LORD, will be their God, and my servant David will rule among them as Prince.' I, the LORD, have spoken this.
>
> **---Ezekiel 34:23-24 (ISV)**

> **(16)** All the people of the land shall give this oblation (offering) for the prince in Israel. **(17)** And it shall be the prince's part to give burnt offerings, and meat offerings, and drink offerings, in the feasts, and in the new moons, and in the Sabbaths, in all solemnities (appointed feasts) of the house of Israel: he shall prepare the sin offering, burnt offering, and the peace offerings, to make reconciliation for the house of Israel.
>
> **---Ezekiel 45:16-17 (KJV)**

Sabbath *(con't)*

If YHWH commanded the Israelites of old to observe the Sabbath and keep His appointed feasts and has shown Ezekiel through prophecy that He will require the house of Israel to observe the Sabbaths and keep His appointed feast during the Millennial Reign, perhaps we should give thought (prayer and meditation) as to what He expects from us as the house of Israel today regarding these things.

Now, let's see what Yeshua said regarding the Sabbath.

> **(1)** At that time Jesus went on the Sabbath day through the corn; and his disciples were an hungered, and began to pluck the ears of corn, and to eat. **(2)** But when the Pharisees saw it, they said unto him, Behold, thy disciples do that which is not lawful to do upon the Sabbath day. **(3)** But He said unto them, Have ye not read what David did, when he was an hungered, and they that were with him; **(4)** How he entered into the house of God, and did eat the showbread, which was not lawful for him to eat, neither for them which were with him, but only for the priests? **(5)** Or have ye not read in the law, how that on the Sabbath days the priests in the temple profane the Sabbath, and are blameless? **(6)** But I say unto you, That in this place is one greater than the temple. **(7)** But if ye had known what this meaneth, I WILL HAVE MERCY, AND NOT SACRIFICE, ye would not have condemned the guiltless. **(8)** For the Son of man is Lord even of the Sabbath day. **(9)** And when he was departed thence, he went into their synagogue: **(10)** And, behold, there was a man which had his hand withered. And they asked him,

Sabbath (con't)

saying, Is it lawful to heal on the Sabbath days? That they might accuse him. **(11)** And he said unto them, What man shall there be among you, that shall have one sheep, and if it fall into a pit on the Sabbath day, will he not lay hold on it, and lift it out? **(12)** How much then is a man better than a sheep? Wherefore it is lawful to do well on the Sabbath days.

---Matthew 12:1-12 (KJV)

1) It was out of necessity that David and his men ate the showbread and Jesus' disciples plucked the ears of corn on the Sabbath day.
2) The Pharisees had created their own "rules and laws" regarding the Sabbath day which allowed them to "profane the Sabbath" and deem themselves blameless.
3) YHWH sent His son, Yeshua, to show us mercy…not requiring daily sacrifices for atonement. Yeshua is our sin sacrifice.
4) Yeshua is greater than the temple.
5) Yeshua declares Himself Lord of the Sabbath day.
6) Yeshua declares that it is lawful to do well on the Sabbath days.
7) Yeshua did not discredit or do away with the Sabbath.

Mark's account of the above events adds:

(27) And he said unto them, The sabbath was made for man, and not man for the sabbath: **(28)** so that the Son of man is lord even of the sabbath.

---Mark 2:27-28 (ASV)

Sabbath (con't)

During Yeshua's description of the sign of His final coming, and of the end of the world, He states:

> **(15)** When ye therefore shall see the ABOMINATION OF DESOLATION, spoken of by Daniel the prophet, stand in the holy place, (whoso readeth, let him understand:) **(16)** Then let them which be in Judea flee into the mountains: **(17)** Let him which is on the housetop not come down to take any thing out of his house: **(18)** Neither let him which is in the field return back to take his clothes. **(19)** And woe unto them that are with child, and to them that give suck in those days! **(20)** But pray ye that your flight be not in the winter, neither on the Sabbath day: **(21)** For then shall be great tribulation, such as was not since the beginning of the world to this time, no, nor ever shall be.
>
> **---Matthew 24:15-21 (KJV)**

Yeshua's description of the End Times tells us when to flee. He tells us to pray that it's not in the winter or on the Sabbath. If this is a prophecy for OUR End Times, does this tell us that we should be observing the Sabbath during OUR End Times?

In John Yeshua speaks of healing on the Sabbath:

> **(19)** Moses gave you the Law, didn't he? Yet none of you is keeping the Law. Why are you trying to kill me?" **(20)** The crowd answered, "You have a demon! Who is trying to kill you?" **(21)** Jesus answered them, "I performed one action, and all of you are astonished. **(22)** Moses gave you circumcision—not that it is from Moses, but from the Patriarchs—and so you circumcise a man on the Sabbath.

Sabbath *(con't)*

> **(23)** If a man receives circumcision on the Sabbath so that the Law of Moses may not be broken, are you angry with me because I made a man perfectly well on the Sabbath?
>
> **---John 7:19-23 (ISV)**

Yeshua reemphasizes that it is lawful to do well on the Sabbath - comparing His healing to the people circumcising a man on the Sabbath just to obey the law of Moses.

The burial of Yeshua.

> **(52)** This man went unto Pilate, and begged the body of Jesus. **(53)** And he took it down, and wrapped it in linen, and laid it in a sepulcher (tomb) that was hewn in stone, wherein never man before was laid. **(54)** And that day was the preparation, and the Sabbath drew on (near). **(55)** And the women also, which came with him from Galilee, followed after, and beheld the sepulcher, and how his body was laid. **(56)** And they returned, and prepared spices and ointments (fragrant oils); and rested the Sabbath day according to the commandment. **(1)** Now upon the first day of the week, very early in the morning, they came unto the sepulcher, bringing the spices which they had prepared, and certain others with them.
>
> **---Luke 23:52-24:1 (KJV)**

Sabbath (con't)

Let us not forget the Ten Commandments, one of which is keeping the Sabbath.

> **(8)** "Remember to keep the Sabbath day holy. **(9)** Six days you are to labor and do all your work, **(10)** but the seventh day is a Sabbath to the LORD your God. You are not to do any work, neither you, nor your son, nor your daughter, nor your male or female servant, nor your livestock, nor the alien who is within your gates, **(11)** because the LORD made the heavens and the earth and the sea, and all that is in them, in six days, then he rested on the seventh day. Therefore, the LORD blessed the Sabbath day and made it holy.
>
> **---Exodus 20:8-11 (ISV)**

> **(12)** Keep the Sabbath day to sanctify it (keep it holy), as the Lord thy God hath commanded thee. **(13)** Six days thou shalt labor, and do all thy work: **(14)** But the seventh day is the Sabbath of the Lord thy God: in it thou shalt not do any work, thou, nor thy son, nor they daughter, nor thy manservant, nor they maidservant, nor thine ox, nor thine ass, nor any of thy cattle, nor thy stranger that is within thy gates; that thy manservant and thy maidservant may rest as well as thou. **(15)** And remember that thou wast a servant in the land of Egypt, and that the Lord thy God brought thee out thence through a mighty hand and by a stretched out arm: therefore the Lord thy God commanded thee to keep (observe) the Sabbath day.
>
> **---Deuteronomy 5:12-15 (KJV)**

Sabbath (con't)

Why do we not observe the Sabbath, which is on our Saturday? *Langenscheidt Pocket Merriam-Webster Dictionary* defines Sabbath as: '1.) the seventh day of the week observed as a day of worship by Jews and some Christians. 2.) Sunday observed among Christians as a day of worship.' {13}

When did Sunday become the Christian day of worship? Did YHWH change it, or man?

As stated in "*The Feasts of Adonai*" by Valerie Moody, from excerpts of various historical writings, the early church observed the Sabbath. Evidence of this can be found in the sources below:

1) The Works of Josephus, Josephus Against Apion, Book 2, Section 40, pg. 811
2) The Whole Works of Jeremy Taylor, Vol. IX, page 416; Gieseler's Church History, vol. 1, Chapter 2, para.
3) Antiquities of the Christian Church, dated 1138, Vol. II, Book XX, Chapter 3, Sec. 1, 66.1137
4) Ancient Christianity Exemplified, Lyman Coleman, Chapter 26, Section 2, page 527

[We begin to see when the observance started to change from YHWH's appointed seventh day of the week to the first day of the week by the following quotes:

> "From the apostles' time until the council of Laodicea, which was about the year 364, the holy observation of the Jew's Sabbath continued, as may be proved out of many authors: yea, notwithstanding the decree of the council against it." *Sunday a Sabbath, by John Ley, London 1640, page 163.*

Sabbath (con't)

> "The seventh-day Sabbath was.. solemnized by Christ, the Apostles, and primitive Christians, till the Laodicean Council did in a manner quite abolish the observation of it." *Dissertation on the Lord's Day, pages 33-34, 44.*

The following is an excerpt from a century-old publication of the Catholic Church:

> "Sunday is a Catholic institution, and its claims to observance can be defended only on Catholic principles... From beginning to end of scripture there is not a single passage that warrants the transfer of weekly public worship from the last day of the week to the first." [cited in] *Catholic Press, Sydney, Australia, August, 1990'*

The following information on the Roman Emperor Constantine is taken from Valerie Moody's "The Feasts of Adonai".

> 'The Roman Emperor Constantine only ruled from 306 to 337, but he profoundly influenced the traditions of the Early Church. He issued the Edict of Milan in 313, giving Christians who worshipped Yeshua the right to worship openly in the Roman Empire. Suddenly, after 200 years of persecution, Christians were free to worship.
>
> On March 7, 321, the Emperor ordered the first National Sunday Law. It stated: "Let all judges and townspeople and occupations of all trades rest on the venerable Day of the Sun."
>
> The name "Day of the Sun" was the festival day of sun worship, our source for the name "Sunday".

Sabbath (con't)

By 324, he declared Christianity to be the official religion of the Roman Empire. We cannot know if Constantine was really a Christian. His goal was to unite the followers of sun worship, the most popular pagan religion, with the followers of Christianity, who worshipped on the Sabbath.

In 325, Constantine presided over the Council of Nicea, which changed the date of the Messiah's resurrection. The Council of Nicea also outlawed all biblical feasts and the Sabbath, which they called "Judaic" practices. Their ultimate goal was to disassociate Christianity from Judaism. They also added pagan holidays.

By 365, The Roman Catholic Church was very much in power. Their Council of Laodicea decided that any Christian keeping the Jewish Sabbath by resting on Saturday instead of Sunday would be excommunicated from the church. A respected Church bishop at the time, John Chrysostom (344 to 407), declared that the Jewish people were the assassins of Christ and worshippers of Satan.] {11}

We can see that YHWH has never changed His Sabbath day from the seventh day (Saturday) to the first day (Sunday) and how important and holy He deemed this special day. From the scriptures, we have learned what it means to hallow and observe YHWH's holy day. It is more than going to church and worshipping Him for a few hours. YHWH honors our worship of Him on days other than His Holy Day, but the majority of us have never been taught, or truly understood what it means to "keep the Sabbath". If YHWH did not change the

Sabbath (con't)

Sabbath to Sunday, but man did, whom do you choose to follow and please…man or YHWH, our Creator?

If we have been unaware of, or have not fully understood YHWH's command to "keep the Sabbath", what else have we been lax in observing that YHWH commands and desires us to do?

Passover
Pesach

Leviticus 23:4 & 5 (KJV) These *are* the feasts of the LORD, *even* holy convocations, which ye shall proclaim in their seasons. In the fourteenth *day* of the first month at even *is* the LORD'S passover.

Origin Date: ***appr. 1447 BC in Egypt***
Originator(s): YHWH (God of Israel)
Description: ***YHWH's First Festival***

(1) And the LORD spake unto Moses and Aaron in the land of Egypt, saying, **(2)** This month *shall be* unto you the beginning of months: it *shall be* the first month of the year to you. **(3)** Speak ye unto all the congregation of Israel, saying, In the tenth *day* of this month they shall take to them every man a lamb, according to the house of *their* fathers, a lamb for an house: **(4)** And if the household be too little for the lamb, let him and his neighbour next unto his house take *it* according to the number of the souls; every man according to his eating shall make your count for the lamb. **(5)** Your lamb shall be without blemish, a male of the first year: ye shall take *it* out from the sheep, or from the goats: **(6)** And ye shall keep it up until the fourteenth day of the same month: and the whole assembly of the congregation of Israel shall kill it in the evening. **(7)** And they shall take of the blood, and strike *it* on the two side posts and on the upper door post of the houses, wherein they shall eat it. **(8)** And they shall eat the flesh in that night, roast with fire, and unleavened

Passover *(con't)*

bread; *and* with bitter *herbs* they shall eat it. **(9)** Eat not of it raw, nor sodden at all with water, but roast *with* fire; his head with his legs, and with the purtenance thereof. **(10)** And ye shall let nothing of it remain until the morning; and that which remaineth of it until the morning ye shall burn with fire. **(11)** And thus shall ye eat it; *with* your loins girded, your shoes on your feet, and your staff in your hand; and ye shall eat it in haste: it *is* the LORD'S passover. **(12)** For I will pass through the land of Egypt this night, and will smite all the firstborn in the land of Egypt, both man and beast; and against all the gods of Egypt I will execute judgment: I *am* the LORD. **(13)** And the blood shall be to you for a token upon the houses where ye *are*: and when I see the blood, I will pass over you, and the plague shall not be upon you to destroy *you*, when I smite the land of Egypt. **(14)** And this day shall be unto you for a memorial; and ye shall keep it a feast to the LORD throughout your generations; ye shall keep it a feast by an ordinance for ever. **(15)** Seven days shall ye eat unleavened bread; even the first day ye shall put away leaven out of your houses: for whosoever eateth leavened bread from the first day until the seventh day, that soul shall be cut off from Israel. **(16)** And in the first day *there shall be* an holy convocation, and in the seventh day there shall be an holy convocation to you; no manner of work shall be done in them, save *that*

Passover *(con't)*

which every man must eat, that only may be done of you. **(17)** And ye shall observe *the feast of* unleavened bread; for in this selfsame day have I brought your armies out of the land of Egypt: therefore shall ye observe this day in your generations by an ordinance for ever. **(18)** In the first *month*, on the fourteenth day of the month at even, ye shall eat unleavened bread, until the one and twentieth day of the month at even. **(19)** Seven days shall there be no leaven found in your houses: for whosoever eateth that which is leavened, even that soul shall be cut off from the congregation of Israel, whether he be a stranger, or born in the land. **(20)** Ye shall eat nothing leavened; in all your habitations shall ye eat unleavened bread. **(21)** Then Moses called for all the elders of Israel, and said unto them, Draw out and take you a lamb according to your families, and kill the passover. **(22)** And ye shall take a bunch of hyssop, and dip *it* in the blood that *is* in the bason, and strike the lintel and the two side posts with the blood that *is* in the bason; and none of you shall go out at the door of his house until the morning. **(23)** For the LORD will pass through to smite the Egyptians; and when he seeth the blood upon the lintel, and on the two side posts, the LORD will pass over the door, and will not suffer the destroyer to come in unto your houses to smite *you*. **(24) And ye shall observe this thing for an ordinance to thee and to thy**

Passover (con't)

sons for ever. **(25)** And it shall come to pass, when ye be come to the land which the LORD will give you, according as he hath promised, that ye shall keep this service. **(26)** And it shall come to pass, when your children shall say unto you, What mean ye by this service? **(27)** That ye shall say, It *is* the sacrifice of the LORD'S passover, who passed over the houses of the children of Israel in Egypt, when he smote the Egyptians, and delivered our houses. And the people bowed the head and worshipped. **(28)** And the children of Israel went away, and did as the LORD had commanded Moses and Aaron, so did they. **(29)** And it came to pass, that at midnight the LORD smote all the firstborn in the land of Egypt, from the firstborn of Pharaoh that sat on his throne unto the firstborn of the captive that *was* in the dungeon; and all the firstborn of cattle. **(30)** And Pharaoh rose up in the night, he, and all his servants, and all the Egyptians; and there was a great cry in Egypt; for *there was* not a house where *there was* not one dead. **(31)** And he called for Moses and Aaron by night, and said, Rise up, *and* get you forth from among my people, both ye and the children of Israel; and go, serve the LORD, as ye have said. **(32)** Also take your flocks and your herds, as ye have said, and be gone; and bless me also. **(33)** And the Egyptians were urgent upon the people, that they might send them out of the land in haste; for they said,

Passover (con't)

We *be* all dead *men*. **(34)** And the people took their
dough before it was leavened, their kneadingtroughs
being bound up in their clothes upon their shoulders.
(35) And the children of Israel did according to the
word of Moses; and they borrowed of the Egyptians
jewels of silver, and jewels of gold, and raiment: **(36)**
And the LORD gave the people favour in the sight of
the Egyptians, so that they lent unto them *such things*
as they required. And they spoiled the Egyptians. **(37)**
And the children of Israel journeyed from Rameses to
Succoth, about six hundred thousand on foot *that were*
men, beside children. **(38)** And a mixed multitude
went up also with them; and flocks, and herds, *even*
very much cattle. **(39)** And they baked unleavened
cakes of the dough which they brought forth out of
Egypt, for it was not leavened; because they were thrust
out of Egypt, and could not tarry, neither had they
prepared for themselves any victual. **(40)** Now the
sojourning of the children of Israel, who dwelt in Egypt,
was four hundred and thirty years. **(41)** And it came
to pass at the end of the four hundred and thirty years,
even the selfsame day it came to pass, that all the hosts
of the LORD went out from the land of Egypt. **(42)** It
is a night to be much observed unto the LORD for
bringing them out from the land of Egypt: this *is* that
night of the LORD to be observed of all the children of
Israel in their generations. **(43)** And the LORD said

Passover (con't)

unto Moses and Aaron, This *is* the ordinance of the passover: There shall no stranger eat thereof: **(44)** But every man's servant that is bought for money, when thou hast circumcised him, then shall he eat thereof. **(45)** A foreigner and an hired servant shall not eat thereof. **(46)** In one house shall it be eaten; thou shalt not carry forth ought of the flesh abroad out of the house; neither shall ye break a bone thereof. **(47)** All the congregation of Israel shall keep it. **(48)** And when a stranger shall sojourn with thee, and will keep the passover to the LORD, let all his males be circumcised, and then let him come near and keep it; and he shall be as one that is born in the land: for no uncircumcised person shall eat thereof. **(49)** **One law shall be to him that is homeborn, and unto the stranger that sojourneth among you.** **(50)** Thus did all the children of Israel; as the LORD commanded Moses and Aaron, so did they. **(51)** And it came to pass the selfsame day, *that* the LORD did bring the children of Israel out of the land of Egypt by their armies.

---Exodus 12:1-51 (KJV)

[**Passover** (Hebrew, Yiddish: פֶּסַח, **Pesach**, Tiberian: pɛsaħ, Israeli: **Pesah**, **Pesakh**, Yiddish: **Peysekh**) is a Jewish and Samaritan holy day and festival commemorating the Exodus from Egypt and the liberation of the Israelites from slavery. It

Passover (con't)

is also known as **Festival of the Unleavened Bread** (חַג הַמַּצּוֹת, ħaɣ ham:asʕ:oθ, "*Chag/Khag Hamatzot/s*").

Passover begins on the 14th day of the month of Nisan, the first month of the Hebrew calendar, in accordance with the Hebrew Bible. The Exodus of the Jews from Egypt took place in the spring and so Passover is celebrated in the spring for seven or eight days.

In the story of Moses, God sent ten plagues upon the Egyptians to convince Pharaoh to release the Israelites. The tenth plague was the killing of the firstborn sons. However, the Israelites were instructed to mark the doorposts of their homes with the blood of a spring lamb, and upon seeing this, the spirit of the Lord passed over these homes, hence the term "passover". When Pharaoh then freed the Israelites, it is said that they left in such a hurry that they could not wait for bread to rise. In commemoration, for the duration of Passover, no leavened bread is eaten, for which reason it is also called "The Festival of the Unleavened Bread". Instead, *matzo* is eaten, and is the primary symbol of the holiday.

Together with Shavuot ("Pentecost") and Sukkot ("Tabernacles"), Passover is one of the three pilgrim festivals (*Shalosh Regalim*) during which the entire Jewish populace historically made a pilgrimage to the Temple in Jerusalem. Samaritans still make this pilgrimage to Mount Gerizim, but only men participate in public worship.] {23}

[In the following passages from Valerie Moody's "The Feasts of Adonai", we see Yeshua's prophetic fulfillment of the Passover Feast:

Passover (con't)

On Passover, Romans crucified Yeshua. He became the Lamb of God who takes away the sins of the world (John 1:29). Yeshua is the Passover lamb. Families selected lambs on Nisan 10 to observe them for four days before Passover. Yeshua entered Jerusalem on Nisan 10, four days before His crucifixion.

At the time of the crucifixion, He breathed His last at 3 pm on Nisan 13. It was the day and hour when men were sacrificing Passover lambs at the Temple. At this very hour, Yeshua paid the price for redemption. Because of Messiah's blood, God's judgment will "pass over" all who believe in Him.

God told the Israelites not to break any of the lamb's bones when they slaughtered it. Not one of Yeshua's bones were broken (Psalm 34:20 and John 19:36). He was led like a lamb to the slaughter, but He did not open His mouth (Isaiah 53:7).] {11}

Today, many believers in YHWH and Yeshua as the Messiah celebrate Passover not only in remembrance of our ancestors being lead from Egypt but also in remembrance of our Savior being the Passover lamb, sacrificed on this day in history. Many believe that those who have the testimony of Yeshua and keep the commandments will in the last days be once again led to a place of protection during the final tribulation days.

Feast of Unleavened Bread
Hag HaMatzah

Leviticus 23:6 (KJV) And on the fifteenth day of the same month *is* the feast of unleavened bread unto the LORD: seven days ye must eat unleavened bread.

Origin Date: ***appr. 1447 BC in Egypt***
Originator(s): YHWH (God of Israel)
Description: ***YHWH's Second Festival***

(1) And the LORD spake unto Moses and Aaron in the land of Egypt, saying, **(2)** This month *shall be* unto you the beginning of months: it *shall be* the first month of the year to you. **(3)** Speak ye unto all the congregation of Israel, saying, In the tenth *day* of this month they shall take to them every man a lamb, according to the house of *their* fathers, a lamb for an house: **(4)** And if the household be too little for the lamb, let him and his neighbour next unto his house take *it* according to the number of the souls; every man according to his eating shall make your count for the lamb. **(5)** Your lamb shall be without blemish, a male of the first year: ye shall take *it* out from the sheep, or from the goats: **(6)** And ye shall keep it up until the fourteenth day of the same month: and the whole assembly of the congregation of Israel shall kill it in the evening. **(7)** And they shall take of the blood, and strike *it* on the two side posts and on the upper door post of the houses, wherein they shall eat it. **(8)** And they shall eat the flesh in that night, roast with fire, and unleavened bread; *and* with bitter *herbs* they shall eat it. **(9)** Eat not of it raw, nor

Feast of Unleavened Bread (con't)

sodden at all with water, but roast *with* fire; his head with his legs, and with the purtenance thereof. **(10)** And ye shall let nothing of it remain until the morning; and that which remaineth of it until the morning ye shall burn with fire. **(11)** And thus shall ye eat it; *with* your loins girded, your shoes on your feet, and your staff in your hand; and ye shall eat it in haste: it *is* the LORD'S passover. **(12)** For I will pass through the land of Egypt this night, and will smite all the firstborn in the land of Egypt, both man and beast; and against all the gods of Egypt I will execute judgment: I *am* the LORD. **(13)** And the blood shall be to you for a token upon the houses where ye *are*: and when I see the blood, I will pass over you, and the plague shall not be upon you to destroy *you*, when I smite the land of Egypt. **(14) And this day shall be unto you for a memorial; and ye shall keep it a feast to the LORD throughout your generations; ye shall keep it a feast by an ordinance for ever.** **(15)** Seven days shall ye eat unleavened bread; even the first day ye shall put away leaven out of your houses: for whosoever eateth leavened bread from the first day until the seventh day, that soul shall be cut off from Israel. **(16)** And in the first day *there shall be* an holy convocation, and in the seventh day there shall be an holy convocation to you; no manner of work shall be done in them, save *that* which every man must eat, that only may be done of you. **(17) And ye**

Feast of Unleavened Bread (con't)

shall observe ***the feast of*** **unleavened bread; for in this selfsame day have I brought your armies out of the land of Egypt: therefore shall ye observe this day in your generations by an ordinance for ever.** **(18)** In the first *month*, on the fourteenth day of the month at even, ye shall eat unleavened bread, until the one and twentieth day of the month at even. **(19)** Seven days shall there be no leaven found in your houses: for whosoever eateth that which is leavened, even that soul shall be cut off from the congregation of Israel, whether he be a stranger, or born in the land. **(20)** Ye shall eat nothing leavened; in all your habitations shall ye eat unleavened bread. **(21)** Then Moses called for all the elders of Israel, and said unto them, Draw out and take you a lamb according to your families, and kill the passover. **(22)** And ye shall take a bunch of hyssop, and dip *it* in the blood that *is* in the bason, and strike the lintel and the two side posts with the blood that *is* in the bason; and none of you shall go out at the door of his house until the morning. **(23)** For the LORD will pass through to smite the Egyptians; and when he seeth the blood upon the lintel, and on the two side posts, the LORD will pass over the door, and will not suffer the destroyer to come in unto your houses to smite *you*. **(24)** **And ye shall observe this thing for an ordinance to thee and to thy sons forever.** **(25)** And it shall come to pass, when ye be come to the land which the LORD will give you, according as he hath promised,

Feast of Unleavened Bread (con't)

that ye shall keep this service. **(26)** And it shall come to pass, when your children shall say unto you, What mean ye by this service? **(27)** That ye shall say, It *is* the sacrifice of the LORD'S passover, who passed over the houses of the children of Israel in Egypt, when he smote the Egyptians, and delivered our houses. And the people bowed the head and worshipped. **(28)** And the children of Israel went away, and did as the LORD had commanded Moses and Aaron, so did they. **(29)** And it came to pass, that at midnight the LORD smote all the firstborn in the land of Egypt, from the firstborn of Pharaoh that sat on his throne unto the firstborn of the captive that *was* in the dungeon; and all the firstborn of cattle. **(30)** And Pharaoh rose up in the night, he, and all his servants, and all the Egyptians; and there was a great cry in Egypt; for *there was* not a house where *there was* not one dead. **(31)** And he called for Moses and Aaron by night, and said, Rise up, *and* get you forth from among my people, both ye and the children of Israel; and go, serve the LORD, as ye have said. **(32)** Also take your flocks and your herds, as ye have said, and be gone; and bless me also. **(33)** And the Egyptians were urgent upon the people, that they might send them out of the land in haste; for they said, We *be* all dead *men*. **(34)** And the people took their dough before it was leavened, their kneadingtroughs being bound up in their clothes upon their shoulders. **(35)** And the children of Israel did according to the word of Moses; and they borrowed of the

Feast of Unleavened Bread (con't)

Egyptians jewels of silver, and jewels of gold, and raiment:
(36) And the LORD gave the people favour in the sight of
the Egyptians, so that they lent unto them *such things as
they required*. And they spoiled the Egyptians. **(37)** And
the children of Israel journeyed from Rameses to Succoth,
about six hundred thousand on foot *that were* men, beside
children. **(38)** And a mixed multitude went up also with
them; and flocks, and herds, *even* very much cattle. **(39)**
And they baked unleavened cakes of the dough which they
brought forth out of Egypt, for it was not leavened; because
they were thrust out of Egypt, and could not tarry, neither
had they prepared for themselves any victual. **(40)** Now
the sojourning of the children of Israel, who dwelt in
Egypt, *was* four hundred and thirty years.

---Exodus 12:1-40 (KJV)

[To observe the Passover and then fail to pursue a sinless life, which is pictured by the Days of Unleavened Bread, would be to fail to understand the meaning of these days and the sacrifice of Christ.

The significance of the Passover and the Festival of Unleavened Bread for the children of God today is clear:

- The seven days of Unleavened Bread picture the process of living a righteous life by observing the laws of God and living a life that is pleasing to him.

Feast of Unleavened Bread (con't)

- In return for eternal and immortal life in the Family and Kingdom of God, each child of God has a covenant with God the Father to pursue a life that is pleasing to him.
- Pursuing a life that is pleasing to the Father requires a continuing effort to reject sin (symbolized by leavened bread) and maintaining purity of thought and righteous behavior (symbolized by unleavened bread).

Putting away leavened products and eating unleavened bread during this seven day festival should do the following:

- Be a reminder of one's sinless condition before God the Father.
- Remind one that the elimination of sin from one's life is a process that takes continual effort.
- Remind one that the internalization of righteous attitudes and behaviors will assure one of eternal and immortal life in the Family and Kingdom of God.

The Festival of Unleavened Bread is a continuation of the spiritual process that began with the observance of the Passover service.

One of the great lessons of the Days of Unleavened Bread is that of becoming and remaining sinless. Remaining in a sinless (unleavened) condition is a lifelong process during which a person must grow toward spiritual maturity (true righteousness). This process only ends when one reaches the end of their life in the human form, which is pictured by the seventh day of the Feast of Unleavened Bread.] {14}

Feast of Firstfruits
HaBikkurim

Leviticus 23:9–11 (KJV) And the LORD spake unto Moses, saying, Speak unto the children of Israel, and say unto them, When ye be come into the land which I give unto you, and shall reap the harvest thereof, then ye shall bring a sheaf of the firstfruits of your harvest unto the priest: And he shall wave the sheaf before the LORD, to be accepted for you: on the morrow after the sabbath the priest shall wave it.

Origin Date: ***appr. 1447 BC at Mt. Sinai***
Originator(s): YHWH (God of Israel)
Description: ***YHWH's Third Festival***

(9) The LORD spoke to Moses, **(10)** "Tell the Israelis that when you enter the land that I'm about to give you and gather its produce, you are to bring a sheaf from the first portion of your harvest to the priest, **(11)** who will offer the sheaf in the LORD's presence for your acceptance. The priest is to wave it on the day after the Sabbath. **(12)** "On the day you wave the sheaf, you are to offer a one year old male lamb without defect for a burnt offering in the LORD's presence. **(13)** Also present a meal offering of two tenths of a measure of fine flour mixed with olive oil as an offering made by fire to the LORD, a pleasing aroma. "Now as to a drink offering, you are to present a fourth of a hin of wine. **(14)** You are not to eat bread, parched grain, or fresh grain until that day when you've brought the offering of your God. This is to be an eternal ordinance throughout your generations, wherever you live."

---Leviticus 23:9-14 (ISV)

Feast of Firstfruits *(con't)*

The third feast occurs during the Feast of Unleavened Bread and is called the Feast of Firstfruits.

Barley is the first crop to be planted in winter, and during this season it is beginning to ripen for its spring harvest. The ripening of the barley is an important event in the Hebraic calendar. The ripening of the barley and the sighting of the new moon determine the beginning of the new year. *Abib* describes the ripeness of the barley. At this point, the barley is brittle and lighter in color.

Until the Hebrews gathered and brought their firstfruits as an offering to the Father, they were not allowed to eat of their harvest. In biblical times a national field of barley was planted near Jerusalem to be observed. Barley was taken from this field and waved in the temple by the High Priest as a firstfruits wave offering before YHWH. After this national offering, each individual family brought their offerings before YHWH. As they handed their baskets of barley and the other required offerings for the day, they would recite Deuteronomy 26:3 and Deuteronomy 26:5-10.

We know that it was during this time that Yeshua was resurrected as a representation of mankind's firstfruit offering before YHWH. John 20:17 tells us that after His resurrection that morning Mary ran to Him and He told her not to touch Him because He hadn't ascended yet. Later in the day, He appeared to His disciples and allowed them to touch Him (Matthew 28:8-10).

Feast of Weeks
Shavuot, Pentecost

Leviticus 23:15-16 (KJV) And ye shall count unto you from the morrow after the sabbath, from the day that ye brought the sheaf of the wave offering; seven sabbaths shall be complete: Even unto the morrow after the seventh sabbath shall ye number fifty days; and ye shall offer a new meat offering unto the LORD.

Origin Date: ***appr. 1447 BC at Mt. Sinai***
Originator(s): YHWH (God of Israel)
Description: ***YHWH's Fourth Festival***

(9) Seven weeks shalt thou number unto thee: begin to number the seven weeks from *such time as* thou beginnest *to put* the sickle to the corn. **(10)** And thou shalt keep the feast of weeks unto the LORD thy God with a tribute of a freewill offering of thine hand, which thou shalt give *unto the LORD thy God*, according as the LORD thy God hath blessed thee: **(11)** And thou shalt rejoice before the LORD thy God, thou, and thy son, and thy daughter, and thy manservant, and thy maidservant, and the Levite that *is* within thy gates, and the stranger, and the fatherless, and the widow, that *are* among you, in the place which the LORD thy God hath chosen to place his name there. **(12)** And thou shalt remember that thou wast a bondman in Egypt: and thou shalt observe and do these statutes.

---Deuteronomy 16:9-12 (KJV)

(15) And ye shall count unto you from the morrow after the sabbath, from the day that ye brought the sheaf of the wave offering; seven sabbaths shall be complete:

Feast of Weeks (con't)

(16) Even unto the morrow after the seventh sabbath shall ye number fifty days; and ye shall offer a new meat offering unto the LORD. **(17)** Ye shall bring out of your habitations two wave loaves of two tenth deals: they shall be of fine flour; they shall be baken with leaven; *they are* the firstfruits unto the LORD. **(18)** And ye shall offer with the bread seven lambs without blemish of the first year, and one young bullock, and two rams: they shall be *for* a burnt offering unto the LORD, with their meat offering, and their drink offerings, *even* an offering made by fire, of sweet savour unto the LORD. **(19)** Then ye shall sacrifice one kid of the goats for a sin offering, and two lambs of the first year for a sacrifice of peace offerings. **(20)** And the priest shall wave them with the bread of the firstfruits *for* a wave offering before the LORD, with the two lambs: they shall be holy to the LORD for the priest. **(21)** And ye shall proclaim on the selfsame day, *that* it may be an holy convocation unto you: ye shall do no servile work *therein: it shall be* a statute for ever in all your dwellings throughout your generations. **(22)** And when ye reap the harvest of your land, thou shalt not make clean riddance of the corners of thy field when thou reapest, neither shalt thou gather any gleaning of thy harvest: thou shalt leave them unto the poor, and to the stranger: I *am* the LORD your God.

---Leviticus 23:15-22 (KJV)

Feast of Weeks (con't)

(1) And it shall be, when thou *art* come in unto the land which the LORD thy God giveth thee *for* an inheritance, and possessest it, and dwellest therein; **(2)** That thou shalt take of the first of all the fruit of the earth, which thou shalt bring of thy land that the LORD thy God giveth thee, and shalt put *it* in a basket, and shalt go unto the place which the LORD thy God shall choose to place his name there. **(3)** And thou shalt go unto the priest that shall be in those days, and say unto him, I profess this day unto the LORD thy God, that I am come unto the country which the LORD sware unto our fathers for to give us. **(4)** And the priest shall take the basket out of thine hand, and set it down before the altar of the LORD thy God. **(5)** And thou shalt speak and say before the LORD thy God, A Syrian ready to perish *was* my father, and he went down into Egypt, and sojourned there with a few, and became there a nation, great, mighty, and populous: **(6)** And the Egyptians evil entreated us, and afflicted us, and laid upon us hard bondage: **(7)** And when we cried unto the LORD God of our fathers, the LORD heard our voice, and looked on our affliction, and our labour, and our oppression: **(8)** And the LORD brought us forth out of Egypt with a mighty hand, and with an outstretched arm, and with great terribleness, and with signs, and with wonders: **(9)** And he hath brought us into this place, and hath given us this land, *even* a land that floweth with milk and honey. **(10)** And now, behold, I have brought the firstfruits of the land, which

Feast of Weeks (con't)

> thou, O LORD, hast given me. And thou shalt set it before the LORD thy God, and worship before the LORD thy God:
> **(11)** And thou shalt rejoice in every good *thing* which the LORD thy God hath given unto thee, and unto thine house, thou, and the Levite, and the stranger that *is* among you.
>
> **---Deuteronomy 26:1-11 (KJV)**

The Feast of Weeks (Shavuot), or better known to the Christian world as Pentecost, is one of the three pilgrimage feasts where all males were required to come to Jerusalem for the festival. This festival is called Pentecost, meaning fiftieth, because there are fifty days between the Feast of Firstfruits and the Feast of Weeks. It was during this feast that the Holy Spirit descended on the disciples and they began to preach to the believers from all nations in their own languages.

The Feast of Weeks is a feast of celebrating the wheat harvest. Pilgrims were to bring their freewill offerings of grain, meat and wine to the temple and present them to the Priest. These offerings were later shared in a joyous feast with the Levites, widows, fatherless and strangers.

Today, Shavuot is also celebrated as the anniversary of the giving of the Torah at Mt. Sinai.

Day of Trumpets
Yom Teruah

Leviticus 23:23-24 (KJV) And the LORD spake unto Moses, saying, Speak unto the children of Israel, saying, In the seventh month, in the first *day* of the month, shall ye have a sabbath, a memorial of blowing of trumpets, an holy convocation.

Origin Date: ***appr. 1447 BC at Mt. Sinai***
Originator(s): YHWH (God of Israel)
Description: ***YHWH's Fifth Festival***

(23) The LORD spoke to Moses, **(24)** Tell the Israelis that on the first day of the seventh month you are to have a Sabbath of rest for you, a memorial announced by a loud blast of trumpets. It is to be a sacred assembly. **(25)** You are not to do any servile work. Instead bring an offering made by fire to the LORD.

---Leviticus 23:23-25 (ISV)

(1) And in the seventh month, on the first *day* of the month, ye shall have an holy convocation; ye shall do no servile work: it is a day of blowing the trumpets unto you. **(2)** And ye shall offer a burnt offering for a sweet savour unto the LORD; one young bullock, one ram, *and* seven lambs of the first year without blemish: **(3)** And their meat offering *shall be of* flour mingled with oil, three tenth deals for a bullock, *and* two tenth deals for a ram, **(4)** And one tenth deal for one lamb, throughout the seven lambs: **(5)** And one kid of the goats *for* a sin offering, to make an

Day of Trumpets *(con't)*

> atonement for you: **(6)** Beside the burnt offering of the month, and his meat offering, and the daily burnt offering, and his meat offering, and their drink offerings, according unto their manner, for a sweet savour, a sacrifice made by fire unto the LORD.
>
> **---Numbers 29:1-6 (KJV)**

[When God established His law, He commanded His people to celebrate seven feasts each year. The feasts were reminders of what God had done for His people and they also represent what YHWH will do at the appointed times. For example, the first four feasts were fulfilled by Christ at the First Coming. The next three feasts will be fulfilled by Christ at His Second Coming. To understand God's future appointed times, let's examine the three remaining feasts.

<u>The Feast of Trumpets</u> is the next feast in God's time-table which will be followed by <u>the Day of Atonement</u> and finally <u>the Feast of Tabernacles</u>. Each feast signifies aspects of what will take place at Christ's Second Coming and the end of the age.

Jesus taught about this final harvest saying, "The field is the world, and the good seed stands for the sons of the kingdom. The weeds are the sons of the evil one, and the enemy who sows them is the devil. The harvest is the end of the age, and the harvesters are angels. … The Son of Man will send out his angels, ..." (Matthew 13:38-39, 41)

In preparation and warning of the coming Feast of Trumpets, the priests would sound trumpets each day. Then at the New

Day of Trumpets (con't)

Moon, the final trumpet blasts signaled the the Feast of Trumpets gathering of Israel to the Temple for the Fall Feast of Ingathering.

On the first day of the seventh month hold a sacred assembly and do no regular work. It is a day for you to sound the trumpets (Deuteronomy 29:1).

At the appointed time of the Feast of Trumpets, the Last Trumpet will signal the gathering of the elect from heaven and earth. Both the Old and New Testaments record information regarding this trumpet call. Below, Jesus describes it in conjunction with His return.

"Immediately after the tribulation of those days "'the sun will be darkened, and the moon will not give its light; the stars will fall from the sky, and the heavenly bodies will be shaken.' "At that time the sign of the Son of Man will appear in the sky, and all the nations of the earth will mourn. They will see the Son of Man coming on the clouds of the sky, with power and great glory. And he will send his angels ***with a loud trumpet call****, and they will gather his elect from the four winds, from one end of the heavens to the other* (Matthew 24:29-31).

Paul wrote about the same thing, referring to the trumpet call and the gathering of believers.

Brothers, we do not want you to be ignorant about those who fall asleep, or to grieve like the rest of men, who have no hope. We believe that Jesus died and rose again and so we believe that God will bring with Jesus those who have fallen asleep in him. According to the Lord's own word, we tell you that we who are still alive, who are left till the coming of the Lord, will

Day of Trumpets (con't)

*certainly not precede those who have fallen asleep. For the Lord himself will come down from heaven, with a loud command, with the voice of the archangel and **with the trumpet call of God**, and the dead in Christ will rise first. After that, we who are still alive and are left will be caught up together with them in the clouds to meet the Lord in the air* (1 Thessalonians 4:13-17).

Years later, Paul wrote to the Church at Corinth a mystery about the last trumpet in connection to the resurrection of the dead and the change in those who would be still alive at the Second Coming.

*Listen, I tell you **a mystery**: We will not all sleep, but we will all be changed-- in a flash, in the twinkling of an eye, **at the last trumpet**. For the trumpet will sound, the dead will be raised imperishable, and we will be changed. For the perishable must clothe itself with the imperishable, and the mortal with immortality* (1 Corinthians 15:51-53).

Under the Old Covenant, Israel would sound daily trumpets of warning leading up to the Feast of Trumpets, when the final trumpet sounded their long blast, Israel would gather in sacred assembly.

In Revelation there is a series of seven trumpets which lead up to the last trumpet. "*And I saw the seven angels who stand before God, and to them were given seven trumpets*" (Revelation 8:2). Then we are told that the mystery will be accomplished when the seventh trumpet sounds.

Day of Trumpets (con't)

*But in the days when **the seventh** angel is about to sound his **trumpet, the mystery** of God will be accomplished, just as he announced to his servants the prophets* (Revelation 10:7)

At the seventh and last trumpet, Christ will begin His reign on earth.

*The **seventh** angel sounded his **trumpet**, and there were loud voices in heaven, which said: "The kingdom of the world has become the kingdom of our Lord and of his Christ, and he will reign for ever and ever." And the twenty-four elders, who were seated on their thrones before God, fell on their faces and worshiped God, saying: "We give thanks to you, Lord God Almighty, the One who is and who was, because you have taken your great power and have begun to reign. The nations were angry; and your wrath has come. The time has come for judging the dead, and for rewarding your servants the prophets and your saints and those who reverence your name, both small and great-- and for destroying those who destroy the earth* (Revelation 11:15-18).

At the last trumpet, Christ will return, establish His Kingdom on earth, judge and reward His saints and punish the unbelieving world.] {15}

Day of Atonement
Yom Kippur

Numbers 29:7 (KJV) And ye shall have on the tenth *day* of this seventh month an holy convocation; and ye shall afflict your souls: ye shall not do any work *therein*:

Origin Date: ***appr. 1447 BC at Mt. Sinai***
Originator(s): ***YHWH (God of Israel)***
Description: ***YHWH's Sixth Festival***

(27) Also on the tenth day of this seventh month *there shall be* a day of atonement: it shall be an holy convocation unto you; and ye shall afflict your souls, and offer an offering made by fire unto the LORD. **(28)** And ye shall do no work in that same day: for it *is* a day of atonement, to make an atonement for you before the LORD your God. **(29)** For whatsoever soul *it be* that shall not be afflicted in that same day, he shall be cut off from among his people. **(30)** And whatsoever soul *it be* that doeth any work in that same day, the same soul will I destroy from among his people. **(31)** Ye shall do no manner of work: *it shall be* **a statute for ever throughout your generations in all your dwellings.** **(32)** It *shall be* unto you a sabbath of rest, and ye shall afflict your souls: in the ninth *day* of the month at even, from even unto even, shall ye celebrate your sabbath.

---Leviticus 23:27-32 (KJV)

Day of Atonement (con't)

(7) And on the tenth day of this seventh month ye shall have a holy convocation; and ye shall afflict your souls: ye shall do no manner of work; (8) but ye shall offer a burnt-offering unto Jehovah for a sweet savor: one young bullock, one ram, seven he-lambs a year old; they shall be unto you without blemish; (9) and their meal-offering, fine flour mingled with oil, three tenth parts for the bullock, two tenth parts for the one ram, (10) a tenth part for every lamb of the seven lambs: (11) one he-goat for a sin-offering; besides the sin-offering of atonement, and the continual burnt-offering, and the meal-offering thereof, and their drink-offerings.

---Numbers 29:7-11 (ASV)

Yom Kippur in Bible Days

[Yom Kippur was the most important day of the year for the High Priest or Cohen HaGadol. This was the only day he stood face to face with God before the Ark of the Covenant to atone for the sins of the people.

An entire chapter of Leviticus is devoted to the service or Avodah of the High Priest on Yom Kippur. Sages even wrote an operations manual for the day! The information occupies an entire tractate or book of the Talmud. The High priest's responsibilities were so important on this day, he appointed a substitute for himself in the event that he could not perform his duties.

Day of Atonement *(con't)*

The High Priest performed Yom Kippur services in all three parts of the Temple – in the courts, the Holy Place, and the Holy of Holies. In the courtyard, he confessed sins, quoted scripture, spoke God's name, and slaughtered animals. In the Holy Place, he cleansed the Altar of Incense. In the Holy of Holies, he sought forgiveness.

For an entire week, the High Priest prepared for Yom Kippur. He left his home and moved to his quarters inside the Temple area seven days early. This kept him from becoming accidentally unclean for the Avodah or service. Twice during the week, the priests cleansed him with the ashes of a red heifer (Numbers 19:1-10). He practiced sacrificing the animals for all Temple services that week, something he normally did not do.

On Yom Kippur, the High Priest conducted four kinds of offerings, the regular daily sacrifice, sin offerings, burnt offerings, and the regular evening sacrifice.

Yeshua the Great High Priest

Aaron may have been the first High Priest of Yom Kippur, but Yeshua is the great High Priest of Yom Kippur. Aaron served until he died; Yeshua is High Priest forever (Hebrews 5:1-6).

The blood of bulls and goats took away Israel's sins for one year. The blood of Yeshua removes sins for all time. "Not with the blood of goats and calves, but with His own blood He entered in the Most Holy Place once for all," (Hebrews 9:12).

Priests burned the animal's bodies outside the camp on Yom Kippur. Yeshua, our Sacrifice, suffered outside the city, too (Hebrews 13:11-12).

Day of Atonement (con't)

Aaron's white linen garments were like Yeshua's garments in Revelation 1:13-15. Aaron alone could minister inside the sacred Holy of Holies. When Roman soldiers sacrificed Yeshua, He suffered and died alone.

Aaron laid aside his beautiful priestly robes on Yom Kippur to wear simple white linen before God. Yeshua, too, laid aside his glory in heaven to come to earth in the likeness of men. Although being like God, he humbled Himself to the point of death (Philippians 2:6-8).

The High Priest on Yom Kippur spoke words similar to Yeshua's words. After he bathed, he asked others not to touch him because he had "not yet ascended" the ramp of the great stone altar to gather hot coals. Yeshua spoke the same words after His resurrection! He said, "Do not keep touching me, for I have not yet ascended to My Father" (John 20:17).

Yeshua served just like the two goats of Yom Kippur. Like the goat for YHWH, He died to sprinkle the Mercy Seat and atone for the sins of the people. Like the goat for Azazel, He carried their sins away.

Aaron's white linen garments were splattered with blood on Yom Kippur. Yeshua's white linen garments will be stained with blood when He returns on Yom Kippur to judge the world and save His people:

> *"I have trodden the winepress...in My anger, and trampled them in My fury; Their blood is sprinkled upon My garments, And I have stained all My robes... He was clothed with a robe dipped in blood, and His name is called The Word of God."*
>
> *Isaiah 63:3 and Revelation 19:13*] {11}

Feast of Tabernacles
Sukkot

Leviticus 23:34-35 (KJV) Speak unto the children of Israel, saying, The fifteenth day of this seventh month *shall be* the feast of tabernacles *for* seven days unto the LORD. On the first day *shall be* an holy convocation: ye shall do no servile work *therein*.

Origin Date: ***appr. 1447 BC at Mt. Sinai***
Originator(s): YHWH (God of Israel)
Description: ***YHWH's Seventh Festival***

(33) And the LORD spake unto Moses, saying, **(34)** Speak unto the children of Israel, saying, The fifteenth day of this seventh month *shall be* the feast of tabernacles *for* seven days unto the LORD. **(35)** On the first day *shall be* an holy convocation: ye shall do no servile work *therein*. **(36)** Seven days ye shall offer an offering made by fire unto the LORD: on the eighth day shall be an holy convocation unto you; and ye shall offer an offering made by fire unto the LORD: it *is* a solemn assembly; *and* ye shall do no servile work *therein*. **(37)** These *are* the feasts of the LORD, which ye shall proclaim *to be* holy convocations, to offer an offering made by fire unto the LORD, a burnt offering, and a meat offering, a sacrifice, and drink offerings, every thing upon his day: **(38)** Beside the sabbaths of the LORD, and beside your gifts, and beside all your vows, and beside all your freewill offerings, which ye give unto the LORD. **(39)** Also in the fifteenth day of the seventh month, when ye have gathered in the fruit of the land, ye shall keep a feast

Feast of Tabernacles (con't)

unto the LORD seven days: on the first day *shall be* a
sabbath, and on the eighth day *shall be* a sabbath. **(40)**
And ye shall take you on the first day the boughs of goodly
trees, branches of palm trees, and the boughs of thick trees,
and willows of the brook; and ye shall rejoice before the
LORD your God seven days. **(41)** And ye shall keep it a
feast unto the LORD seven days in the year. *It shall be* a
statute for ever in your generations: ye shall celebrate it in
the seventh month. **(42)** Ye shall dwell in booths seven
days; all that are Israelites born shall dwell in booths:
(43) That your generations may know that I made the
children of Israel to dwell in booths, when I brought them
out of the land of Egypt: I *am* the LORD your God. **(44)**
And Moses declared unto the children of Israel the feasts of
the LORD.

---Leviticus 23:33-44 (KJV)

(13) Thou shalt observe the feast of tabernacles seven
days, after that thou hast gathered in thy corn and thy
wine: **(14)** And thou shalt rejoice in thy feast, thou, and
thy son, and thy daughter, and thy manservant, and thy
maidservant, and the Levite, the stranger, and the
fatherless, and the widow, that *are* within thy gates. **(15)**
Seven days shalt thou keep a solemn feast unto the LORD
thy God in the place which the LORD shall choose: because
the LORD thy God shall bless thee in all thine increase, and
in all the works of thine hands, therefore thou shalt surely
rejoice. **(16)** Three times in a year shall all thy males

Feast of Tabernacles (con't)

appear before the LORD thy God in the place which he shall choose; in the feast of unleavened bread, and in the feast of weeks, and in the feast of tabernacles: and they shall not appear before the LORD empty: **(17)** Every man *shall give* as he is able, according to the blessing of the LORD thy God which he hath given thee. (18) Judges and officers shalt thou make thee in all thy gates, which the LORD thy God giveth thee, throughout thy tribes: and they shall judge the people with just judgment. (19) Thou shalt not wrest judgment; thou shalt not respect persons, neither take a gift: for a gift doth blind the eyes of the wise, and pervert the words of the righteous. **(20)** That which is altogether just shalt thou follow, that thou mayest live, and inherit the land which the LORD thy God giveth thee. **(21)** Thou shalt not plant thee a grove of any trees near unto the altar of the LORD thy God, which thou shalt make thee. **(22)** Neither shalt thou set thee up *any* image; which the LORD thy God hateth.

---Deuteronomy 16:13-22 (KJV)

(10) Then he gave these orders: "At the end of seven years, the year designated for release, during the Feast of Tents, **(11)** when all of Israel comes to appear in the presence of the LORD your God at the place that he'll choose, read this Law aloud to them.

---Deuteronomy 31:10-11 (ISV)

Feast of Tabernacles (con't)

[Sukkot was agricultural in origin. This is evident from the name "The Feast of Ingathering," from the ceremonies accompanying it, and from the season and occasion of its celebration: "At the end of the year when you gather in your labors out of the field" (Ex. 23:16); "after you have gathered in from your threshing-floor and from your winepress" (Deut. 16:13). It was a thanksgiving for the fruit harvest (compare Judges 9:27). And in what may explain the festival's name, Isaiah reports that grape harvesters kept booths in their vineyards (Isa. 1:8). Coming as it did at the completion of the harvest, Sukkot was regarded as a general thanksgiving for the bounty of nature in the year that had passed.

Sukkot became one of the most important feasts in Judaism, as indicated by its designation as "the Feast of the Lord" (Lev. 23:39; Judges 21:19) or simply "the Feast" (1 Kings 8:2, 65; 12:32; 2 Chron. 5:3, 7:8). Perhaps because of its wide attendance, Sukkot became the appropriate time for important state ceremonies. Moses instructed the children of Israel to gather for a reading of the Law during Sukkot every seventh year (Deut. 31:10-11). King Solomon dedicated the Temple in Jerusalem on Sukkot (1 Kings 8; 2 Chron. 7). And Sukkot was the first sacred occasion observed after the resumption of sacrifices in Jerusalem after the Babylonian captivity (Ezra 3:2-4).

In the time of Nehemiah, after the Babylonian captivity, the Israelites celebrated Sukkot by making and dwelling in booths, a practice of which Nehemiah reports: "the Israelites had not done so from the days of Joshua" (Neh. 8:13-17). In a practice related to that of the Four Species, Nehemiah also reports that the Israelites found in the Law the commandment that they "go out to the mountains and bring leafy branches of olive trees,

Feast of Tabernacles (con't)

pine trees, myrtles, palms and (other) leafy trees to make booths" (Neh. 8:14-15). In Leviticus, God told Moses to command the people: "On the first day you shall take the product of *hadar* trees, branches of palm trees, boughs of leafy trees, and willows of the brook" (Lev. 23:40), and "You shall live in booths seven days; all citizens in Israel shall live in booths, in order that future generations may know that I made the Israelite people live in booths when I brought them out of the land of Egypt" (Lev. 23:42-43). Numbers, however, indicates that while in the wilderness, the Israelites dwelt in tents (Num. 11:10, 16:27). Some secular scholars consider Leviticus 23:39-43 (the commandments regarding booths and the four species) to be an insertion by a late redactor. (E.g., Richard Elliott Friedman. *The Bible with Sources Revealed*, 228-29. New York: HarperSanFranciso, 2003.)

Jeroboam son of Nebat, King of the northern Kingdom of Israel, whom Kings describes as practicing "his evil way" (1 Kings 13:33), celebrated a festival on the fifteenth day of the eighth month, one month after Sukkot, "in imitation of the festival in Judah" (1 Kings 12:32-33). "While Jeroboam was standing on the altar to present the offering, the man of God, at the command of the Lord, cried out against the altar" in disapproval (1 Kings 13:1).

According to Zechariah (Zech 14:16-19), Sukkot in the messianic era will become a universal festival, and all nations will make pilgrimages annually to Jerusalem to celebrate the feast there. (A modern interpretation of this resulted in a recent holiday celebrated in Jerusalem by non-Jews, "The Feast of Tabernacles".) Sukkot is here associated with the granting of rain, an idea further developed in later Jewish literature.] {24}

Feast of Tabernacles (con't)

Did Yeshua observe Feast of Tabernacles?
[Christian observers point out that Jesus kept the Feast of Tabernacles. This is discussed in detail in John chapter 7:10-26:

> But when His brothers had gone up, then He also went up to the feast, not openly, but as it were in secret. Then the Jews sought Him at the feast, and said, "Where is He?" And there was much complaining among the people concerning Him. Some said, "He is good"; others said, "No, on the contrary, he deceives the people." However, no one spoke openly of Him for fear of the Jews. Now about the middle of the feast Jesus went up into the temple and taught. And the Jews marveled, saying, "How does this Man know letter, having never studied?" Jesus answered them and said, "My doctrine is not Mine, but His who sent Me. If anyone wants to do His will, he shall know concerning the doctrine, whether it is from God or whether I speak on My own authority. He who speaks from himself seeks his own glory; but He who seeks the glory of the One who sent Him is true, and no unrighteousness is in Him. Did not Moses give you the law, yet none of you keeps the law? Why do you seek to kill Me?"
>
> The people answered and said, "You have a demon. Who is seeking to kill You?" Jesus answered and said to them, "I did one work, and you all marvel. Moses therefore gave you circumcision (not that it is from Moses, but from the fathers), and you circumcise a man on the Sabbath. If a man receives circumcision on the Sabbath, so that the law of Moses should not be broken,

Feast of Tabernacles (con't)

> are you angry with Me because I made a man completely well on the Sabbath? Do not judge according to appearance, but judge with righteous judgment." Now some of them from Jerusalem said, "Is this not He whom they seek to kill? But look! He speaks boldly, and they say nothing to Him. Do the rulers know indeed that this is truly the Christ?"

The issue of how non-Jewish Christians related to Jewish Christians was a very serious issue in the early church. Jesus and all his first followers were Jewish. However, from the Biblical and extra-biblical evidence, only a short time elapsed before non-Jewish people became convinced that Jesus was the Jewish Messiah. For Gentiles coming to a Jewish messiah, the issue of what was essential for them to adopt and what was (legitimate but) optional Jewish custom amongst the Jewish followers of Jesus Christ came to the fore. It is significant that the (Jewish) Apostle Paul himself kept the Feast of Tabernacles. As it is noted in Acts 18:21: "I must by all means keep this coming feast in Jerusalem; but I will return again to you, God willing."] {25}

Will we be commanded to celebrate the Feast of Tabernacles in the future?
The following prophecy of OUR future as seen by Zechariah:

> **(1)** Behold, the day of the LORD cometh, and thy spoil shall be divided in the midst of thee. **(2)** For I will gather all nations against Jerusalem to battle; and the city shall be taken, and the houses rifled, and the women ravished; and half of the city shall go forth into captivity, and the residue of the people shall not be cut off from the city.

Feast of Tabernacles (con't)

(3) Then shall the LORD go forth, and fight against those nations, as when he fought in the day of battle. **(4)** And his feet shall stand in that day upon the mount of Olives, which *is* before Jerusalem on the east, and the mount of Olives shall cleave in the midst thereof toward the east and toward the west, *and there shall be* a very great valley; and half of the mountain shall remove toward the north, and half of it toward the south. **(5)** And ye shall flee *to* the valley of the mountains; for the valley of the mountains shall reach unto Azal: yea, ye shall flee, like as ye fled from before the earthquake in the days of Uzziah king of Judah: and the LORD my God shall come, *and* all the saints with thee. **(6)** And it shall come to pass in that day, *that* the light shall not be clear, *nor* dark: **(7)** But it shall be one day which shall be known to the LORD, not day, nor night: but it shall come to pass, *that* at evening time it shall be light. **(8)** And it shall be in that day, *that* living waters shall go out from Jerusalem; half of them toward the former sea, and half of them toward the hinder sea: in summer and in winter shall it be. **(9)** And the LORD shall be king over all the earth: in that day shall there be one LORD, and his name one. **(10)** All the land shall be turned as a plain from Geba to Rimmon south of Jerusalem: and it shall be lifted up, and inhabited in her place, from Benjamin's gate unto the place of the first gate, unto the corner gate, and *from* the tower of Hananeel unto the king's winepresses. **(11)** And *men* shall dwell in it, and there shall be no more utter

Feast of Tabernacles (con't)

destruction; but Jerusalem shall be safely inhabited. (12) And this shall be the plague wherewith the LORD will smite all the people that have fought against Jerusalem; Their flesh shall consume away while they stand upon their feet, and their eyes shall consume away in their holes, and their tongue shall consume away in their mouth. (13) And it shall come to pass in that day, *that* a great tumult from the LORD shall be among them; and they shall lay hold every one on the hand of his neighbour, and his hand shall rise up against the hand of his neighbour. (14) And Judah also shall fight at Jerusalem; and the wealth of all the heathen round about shall be gathered together, gold, and silver, and apparel, in great abundance. (15) And so shall be the plague of the horse, of the mule, of the camel, and of the ass, and of all the beasts that shall be in these tents, as this plague. **(16) And it shall come to pass, *that* every one that is left of all the nations which came against Jerusalem shall even go up from year to year to worship the King, the LORD of hosts, and to keep the feast of tabernacles. (17) And it shall be, *that* whoso will not come up of *all* the families of the earth unto Jerusalem to worship the King, the LORD of hosts, even upon them shall be no rain. (18) And if the family of Egypt go not up, and come not, that *have* no *rain*; there shall be the plague, wherewith the LORD will smite the heathen that come not up to keep the feast of**

Feast of Tabernacles *(con't)*

> **tabernacles. (19) This shall be the punishment of Egypt, and the punishment of all nations that come not up to keep the feast of tabernacles.** (20) In that day shall there be upon the bells of the horses, HOLINESS UNTO THE LORD; and the pots in the LORD'S house shall be like the bowls before the altar. (21) Yea, every pot in Jerusalem and in Judah shall be holiness unto the LORD of hosts: and all they that sacrifice shall come and take of them, and seethe therein: and in that day there shall be no more the Canaanite in the house of the LORD of hosts.
>
> **---Zechariah 14:1-21 (KJV)**

The Feast of Tabernacles (Sukkot) has always included Gentiles. The entire "household" will see the Heavenly Father "tabernacle" with us on the earth:

> (1) And I saw a new heaven and a new earth: for the first heaven and the first earth were passed away; and there was no more sea. (2) And I John saw the holy city, new Jerusalem, coming down from God out of heaven, prepared as a bride adorned for her husband. (3) And I heard a great voice out of heaven saying, Behold, the tabernacle of God *is* with men, and he will dwell with them, and they shall be his people, and God himself shall be with them, *and be* their God.
>
> **---Revelation 21:1-3 (KJV)**

Feast of Dedication
Hanukkah

John 10:22-23 (KJV) And it was at Jerusalem the feast of the dedication, and it was winter. And Jesus walked in the temple in Solomon's porch.

Origin Date: appr 165 BC
Originator(s): Israelites
Description: Feast of the People in honor of the rededication of the Temple in 165 BC after it's capture and desecration by Antiochus IV Epiphanes.

The books of I & II Maccabees (uncanonized writings from appr. 100 BC) describe the struggle the Israelite people went through during the rule of Antiochus IV Epiphanes in 175 BC.

Antiochus IV Epiphanes was a Greek king who forced the Jewish people to give up their way of worship and beliefs and begin worshipping Greek gods.

He turned the temple in Jerusalem into a temple for Zeus, the Greek god. He ordered the Jewish people to make sacrifices to the Greek deities. He desecrated the Temple by setting up an "abomination of desolation" as described in Daniel 11. This "abomination of desolation" was a Greek idol. It is interesting to note that Antiochus ruled for 3.5 years. This is the same period of time it is prophesied for the Antichrist to rule. Yeshua Himself tells us beginning in Mathew 24:15 (and again beginning in Mark 24:15) that this will again occur. He warns those in Judaea to flee to the mountains in haste and to pray that their exodus is not in the winter!

The cruelty of Antiochus and his demise is told in the following verses of I Maccabees, Chapters 1 & 2.

Feast of Dedication *(con't)*

(10) And there came out of them a wicked root Antiochus *surnamed* Epiphanes, son of Antiochus the king, who had been an hostage at Rome, and he reigned in the hundred and thirty and seventh year of the kingdom of the Greeks. **(11)** In those days went there out of Israel wicked men, who persuaded many, saying, Let us go and make a covenant with the heathen that are round about us: for since we departed from them we have had much sorrow. **(12)** So this device pleased them well. **(13)** Then certain of the people were so forward herein, that they went to the king, who gave them licence to do after the ordinances of the heathen: **(14)** Whereupon they built a place of exercise at Jerusalem according to the customs of the heathen: **(15)** And made themselves uncircumcised, and forsook the holy covenant, and joined themselves to the heathen, and were sold to do mischief.

---I Maccabee 1:10-15

We can't entirely blame Antiochus in the beginning! Many of the Israelites desired to join themselves to the heathen and take on their ways even to the point of forsaking the holy covenant! We should pay attention to this historical event as scripture foretells it happening again!

(20) And after that Antiochus had smitten Egypt, he returned again in the hundred forty and third year, and went up against Israel and Jerusalem with a great

Feast of Dedication (con't)

multitude, **(21)** And entered proudly into the sanctuary, and took away the golden altar, and the candlestick of light, and all the vessels thereof, **(22)** And the table of the shewbread, and the pouring vessels, and the vials. and the censers of gold, and the veil, and the crown, and the golden ornaments that were before the temple, all which he pulled off. **(23)** He took also the silver and the gold, and the precious vessels: also he took the hidden treasures which he found. **(24)** And when he had taken all away, he went into his own land, having made a great massacre, and spoken very proudly. **(25)** Therefore there was a great mourning in Israel, in every place where they were; **(26)** So that the princes and elders mourned, the virgins and young men were made feeble, and the beauty of women was changed. **(27)** Every bridegroom took up lamentation, and she that sat in the marriage chamber was in heaviness, **(28)** The land also was moved for the inhabitants thereof, and all the house of Jacob was covered with confusion. **(29)** And after two years fully expired the king sent his chief collector of tribute unto the cities of Juda, who came unto Jerusalem with a great multitude, **(30)** And spake peaceable words unto them, but all was deceit: for when they had given him credence, he fell suddenly upon the city, and smote it very sore, and destroyed much people of Israel. **(31)** And when he had taken the spoils of the city, he set it on fire, and pulled down the houses and walls thereof on every side. **(32)** But the women and children

Feast of Dedication (con't)

took they captive, and possessed the cattle. **(33)** Then builded they the city of David with a great and strong wall, and with mighty towers, and made it a strong hold for them. **(34)** And they put therein a sinful nation, wicked men, and fortified themselves therein. **(35)** They stored it also with armour and victuals, and when they had gathered together the spoils of Jerusalem, they laid them up there, and so they became a sore snare: **(36)** For it was a place to lie in wait against the sanctuary, and an evil adversary to Israel. **(37)** Thus they shed innocent blood on every side of the sanctuary, and defiled it: **(38)** Insomuch that the inhabitants of Jerusalem fled because of them: whereupon the city was made an habitation of strangers, and became strange to those that were born in her; and her own children left her. **(39)** Her sanctuary was laid waste like a wilderness, her feasts were turned into mourning, her sabbaths into reproach her honour into contempt. **(40)** As had been her glory, so was her dishonour increased, and her excellency was turned into mourning. **(41)** Moreover king Antiochus wrote to his whole kingdom, that all should be one people, **(42)** And every one should leave his laws: so all the heathen agreed according to the commandment of the king. **(43)** Yea, many also of the Israelites consented to his religion, and sacrificed unto idols, and profaned the sabbath. **(44)** For the king had sent letters by messengers unto Jerusalem and the cities of Juda that they should follow the strange laws of the land, **(45)** And

Feast of Dedication (con't)

forbid burnt offerings, and sacrifice, and drink offerings, in the temple; and that they should profane the sabbaths and festival days: **(46)** And pollute the sanctuary and holy people: **(47)** Set up altars, and groves, and chapels of idols, and sacrifice swine's flesh, and unclean beasts: **(48)** That they should also leave their children uncircumcised, and make their souls abominable with all manner of uncleanness and profanation: **(49)** To the end they might forget the law, and change all the ordinances. **(50)** And whosoever would not do according to the commandment of the king, he said, he should die. **(51)** In the selfsame manner wrote he to his whole kingdom, and appointed overseers over all the people, commanding the cities of Juda to sacrifice, city by city. **(52)** Then many of the people were gathered unto them, to wit every one that forsook the law; and so they committed evils in the land; **(53)** And drove the Israelites into secret places, even wheresoever they could flee for succour. **(54)** Now the fifteenth day of the month Casleu, in the hundred forty and fifth year, they set up the abomination of desolation upon the altar, and builded idol altars throughout the cities of Juda on every side; **(55)** And burnt incense at the doors of their houses, and in the streets. **(56)** And when they had rent in pieces the books of the law which they found, they burnt them with fire. **(57)** And whosoever was found with any the book of the testament, or if any committed to the law, the king's commandment was, that they should

Feast of Dedication (con't)

put him to death. **(58)** Thus did they by their authority unto the Israelites every month, to as many as were found in the cities. **(59)** Now the five and twentieth day of the month they did sacrifice upon the idol altar, which was upon the altar of God. **(60)** At which time according to the commandment they put to death certain women, that had caused their children to be circumcised. **(61)** And they hanged the infants about their necks, and rifled their houses, and slew them that had circumcised them. **(62)** Howbeit many in Israel were fully resolved and confirmed in themselves not to eat any unclean thing. **(63)** Wherefore the rather to die, that they might not be defiled with meats, and that they might not profane the holy covenant: so then they died. **(64)** And there was very great wrath upon Israel. {37}

---I Maccabee 1:20-64

Finally, YHWH-fearing, Torah observing, men rise up to stand against the heathen and those who have joined themselves to them to defend the Father's ways!

(1) In those days arose Mattathias the son of John, the son of Simeon, a priest of the sons of Joarib, from Jerusalem, and dwelt in Modin. **(2)** And he had five sons, Joannan, called Caddis: **(3)** Simon; called Thassi: **(4)** Judas, who was called Maccabeus: **(5)** Eleazar, called Avaran: and Jonathan, whose surname was Apphus. **(6)** And when he

Feast of Dedication (con't)

saw the blasphemies that were committed in Juda and Jerusalem, **(7)** He said, Woe is me! wherefore was I born to see this misery of my people, and of the holy city, and to dwell there, when it was delivered into the hand of the enemy, and the sanctuary into the hand of strangers? **(8)** Her temple is become as a man without glory. **(9)** Her glorious vessels are carried away into captivity, her infants are slain in the streets, her young men with the sword of the enemy. **(10)** What nation hath not had a part in her kingdom and gotten of her spoils? **(11)** All her ornaments are taken away; of a free woman she is become a bondslave. **(12)** And, behold, our sanctuary, even our beauty and our glory, is laid waste, and the Gentiles have profaned it. **(13)** To what end therefore shall we live any longer? **(14)** Then Mattathias and his sons rent their clothes, and put on sackcloth, and mourned very sore. **(15)** In the mean while the king's officers, such as compelled the people to revolt, came into the city Modin, to make them sacrifice. **(16)** And when many of Israel came unto them, Mattathias also and his sons came together. **(17)** Then answered the king's officers, and said to Mattathias on this wise, Thou art a ruler, and an honourable and great man in this city, and strengthened with sons and brethren: **(18)** Now therefore come thou first, and fulfil the king's commandment, like as all the heathen have done, yea, and the men of Juda also, and such as remain at Jerusalem: so shalt thou and thy house

Feast of Dedication (con't)

be in the number of the king's friends, and thou and thy children shall be honoured with silver and gold, and many rewards. **(19)** Then Mattathias answered and spake with a loud voice, Though all the nations that are under the king's dominion obey him, and fall away every one from the religion of their fathers, and give consent to his commandments: **(20)** Yet will I and my sons and my brethren walk in the covenant of our fathers. **(21)** God forbid that we should forsake the law and the ordinances. **(22)** We will not hearken to the king's words, to go from our religion, either on the right hand, or the left. **(23)** Now when he had left speaking these words, there came one of the Jews in the sight of all to sacrifice on the altar which was at Modin, according to the king's commandment. **(24)** Which thing when Mattathias saw, he was inflamed with zeal, and his reins trembled, neither could he forbear to shew his anger according to judgment: wherefore he ran, and slew him upon the altar. **(25)** Also the king's commissioner, who compelled men to sacrifice, he killed at that time, and the altar he pulled down. **(26)** Thus dealt he zealously for the law of God like as Phinees did unto Zambri the son of Salom. **(27)** And Mattathias cried throughout the city with a loud voice, saying, Whosoever is zealous of the law, and maintaineth the covenant, let him follow me. **(28)** So he and his sons fled into the mountains, and left all that ever they had in the city. **(29)** Then many that sought after justice and judgment went

Feast of Dedication (con't)

down into the wilderness, to dwell there: **(30)** Both they, and their children, and their wives; and their cattle; because afflictions increased sore upon them. **(31)** Now when it was told the king's servants, and the host that was at Jerusalem, in the city of David, that certain men, who had broken the king's commandment, were gone down into the secret places in the wilderness, **(32)** They pursued after them a great number, and having overtaken them, they camped against them, and made war against them on the sabbath day. **(33)** And they said unto them, Let that which ye have done hitherto suffice; come forth, and do according to the commandment of the king, and ye shall live. **(34)** But they said, We will not come forth, neither will we do the king's commandment, to profane the sabbath day. **(35)** So then they gave them the battle with all speed. **(36)** Howbeit they answered them not, neither cast they a stone at them, nor stopped the places where they lay hid; **(37)** But said, Let us die all in our innocency: heaven and earth will testify for us, that ye put us to death wrongfully. **(38)** So they rose up against them in battle on the sabbath, and they slew them, with their wives and children and their cattle, to the number of a thousand people. **(39)** Now when Mattathias and his friends understood hereof, they mourned for them right sore. **(40)** And one of them said to another, If we all do as our brethren have done, and fight not for our lives and laws against the heathen, they will now quickly root us out of

Feast of Dedication (con't)

the earth. **(41)** At that time therefore they decreed, saying, Whosoever shall come to make battle with us on the sabbath day, we will fight against him; neither will we die all, as our brethren that were murdered in the secret places. **(42)** Then came there unto him a company of Assideans who were mighty men of Israel, even all such as were voluntarily devoted unto the law. **(43)** Also all they that fled for persecution joined themselves unto them, and were a stay unto them. **(44)** So they joined their forces, and smote sinful men in their anger, and wicked men in their wrath: but the rest fled to the heathen for succour. **(45)** Then Mattathias and his friends went round about, and pulled down the altars: **(46)** And what children soever they found within the coast of Israel uncircumcised, those they circumcised valiantly. **(47)** They pursued also after the proud men, and the work prospered in their hand. **(48)** So they recovered the law out of the hand of the Gentiles, and out of the hand of kings, neither suffered they the sinner to triumph. **(49)** Now when the time drew near that Mattathias should die, he said unto his sons, Now hath pride and rebuke gotten strength, and the time of destruction, and the wrath of indignation: **(50)** Now therefore, my sons, be ye zealous for the law, and give your lives for the covenant of your fathers. **(51)** Call to remembrance what acts our fathers did in their time; so shall ye receive great honour and an everlasting name. **(52)** Was not Abraham found faithful in temptation, and it

Feast of Dedication (con't)

was imputed unto him for righteousness? **(53)** Joseph in the time of his distress kept the commandment and was made lord of Egypt. **(54)** Phinees our father in being zealous and fervent obtained the covenant of an everlasting priesthood. **(55)** Jesus for fulfilling the word was made a judge in Israel. **(56)** Caleb for bearing witness before the congregation received the heritage of the land. **(57)** David for being merciful possessed the throne of an everlasting kingdom. **(58)** Elias for being zealous and fervent for the law was taken up into heaven. **(59)** Ananias, Azarias, and Misael, by believing were saved out of the flame. **(60)** Daniel for his innocency was delivered from the mouth of lions. **(61)** And thus consider ye throughout all ages, that none that put their trust in him shall be overcome. **(62)** Fear not then the words of a sinful man: for his glory shall be dung and worms. **(63)** To day he shall be lifted up and tomorrow he shall not be found, because he is returned into his dust, and his thought is come to nothing. **(64)** Wherefore, ye my sons, be valiant and shew yourselves men in the behalf of the law; for by it shall ye obtain glory. **(65)** And behold, I know that your brother Simon is a man of counsel, give ear unto him alway: he shall be a father unto you. **(66)** As for Judas Maccabeus, he hath been mighty and strong, even from his youth up: let him be your captain, and fight the battle of the people. **(67)** Take also unto you all those that observe the law, and avenge ye the wrong of your people. **(68)** Recompense fully the heathen,

Feast of Dedication (con't)

> and take heed to the commandments of the law. **(69)** So he blessed them, and was gathered to his fathers. **(70)** And he died in the hundred forty and sixth year, and his sons buried him in the sepulchres of his fathers at Modin, and all Israel made great lamentation for him. {37}
>
> **---I Maccabee 2:1-70**

This Feast of Dedication declared by the people is celebrated in remembrance of the victory of a small army of Israelites who took a stand for their faith, their Holy Father and His way of life.

Today Hanukkah is celebrated with many added traditions. One traditional story tells us that the miracle of the olive oil happened during this time. Historical records, including Josephus, do not mention this miracle occurring at the time of the rededication. The story states that there was only enough oil to burn in the temple's menorah for one day. The story goes on to say that when the Israelites lit the oil in the menorah; it miraculously burned for eight days, which is the amount of time it takes to refine and sanctify oil for use in the temple.

The use of a hanukkiah, a nine-branch menorah, has long been a traditional part of Hanukkah celebrations. However, there is no scriptural reference of the nine-branch candlestick. There is

Feast of Dedication (con't)

also no mention of lighting candles and giving gifts during this festival in scripture.

Another tradition for Hanukkah is playing the dreidel game. [Dreidel is a four-sided top that has different letters painted on each of its side. With one letter on each side, they make up the acronym for the phrase, "A great miracle happened there."

Why is this game so linked with Hanukkah? During the rule of the Greek-Syrians, studying the Torah was outlawed and if anyone was caught, the "crime" was punishable by death. So, when the children were studying the Torah and they saw a Greek patrol come by, they would quickly hide the Torah and take out a dreidel and began playing. So it is a reminder of the brave children who had the courage to study the Torah even during such dangerous times.] {16}

In researching Saturnalia which occurs during the winter solstice, we must be mindful of how this festival to honor the dedication of the temple to Saturn is observed. This celebration continues today. The similarities with today's traditional observance of Hanukkah are: candles and gifts. Saturnalia is observed for seven days. We must be careful not to blend the observances of this pagan holiday with the observance of a memorial of Israel.

[Saturnalia is the feast with which the Romans commemorated the dedication of the temple of the god Saturn, which was on December 17. Over the years, it expanded to a whole week, to December 23.

Feast of Dedication (con't)

Saturnalia became one of the most popular Roman festivals. It was marked by tomfoolery and reversal of social roles, in which slaves and masters ostensibly switched places.] {38}

We must remember to be careful in observing man's traditions blended in with the Father's Holy Days. Although Hanukkah is not a Feast declared by the Father, it is a memorial to those in the faith that have so valiantly stood up for and defended the Father's commandments. Hanukkah in no way should be elevated to the same status of the Father's Holy Days as commanded in scripture.

Holy Days Observations

In researching the history of these Holy Days, we have come to the following conclusions:

1) The Holy Days mentioned were originated by YHWH Himself with the exception of Hanukkah which is a festival of the people. There are other festivals of the people celebrated and recognized by the nation of Israel not mentioned in this material. The festivals originated by YHWH are detailed in the Holy Scriptures given to Israel and it's generations to come. Some were described as everlasting covenants and to be observed "forever".
2) Even these Holy Days described in Scripture have been added to or taken away from by man incorporating his traditions and customs. That is why we must be very careful to follow Scripture as best we can and pray for the Spirit's guidance and revelation in how we should observe these festivals. Since Yeshua's sacrifice and the destruction of the temple, we do not observe the sacrificial offering as described in Scripture. Ezekiel tells us that during the millennial reign the sacrifices will begin once again at the rebuilt temple.

Holy Days Observations (con't)

When Yeshua walked the earth and dwelt among us, He openly rebuked the Pharisees for adding to and/or taking away from His Father's Word, His Word.

(7) Their worship of me is worthless, because they teach human rules as doctrines.' **(8)** You abandon the commandment of God and hold to human tradition." **(9)** Then he told them, "You have such a fine way of rejecting the commandment of God in order to keep your own tradition!

---Mark 7:7-9 (ISV)

3) All of the Holy Days we have mentioned in the above material were observed by Yeshua Himself and His disciples. We know that He is our perfect example!

(25) The one who loves his life will destroy it, and the one who hates his life in this world will preserve it for eternal life. **(26)** If anyone serves me, he must follow me. And where I am, there my servant will also be. If anyone serves me, the Father will honor him."

---John 12:25-26 (ISV)

Yeshua came to be an example to us, bless us, redeem us by His sacrifice and turn us away from our iniquities (lawlessness).

(22) For Moses truly said unto the fathers, A prophet shall the Lord your God raise up unto you of your brethren, like unto me; him shall ye hear in all things whatsoever he shall

Holy Days Observations (con't)

say unto you. **(23)** And it shall come to pass, *that* every soul, which will not hear that prophet, shall be destroyed from among the people. **(24)** Yea, and all the prophets from Samuel and those that follow after, as many as have spoken, have likewise foretold of these days. **(25)** Ye are the children of the prophets, and of the covenant which God made with our fathers, saying unto Abraham, And in thy seed shall all the kindreds of the earth be blessed. **(26)** Unto you first God, having raised up his Son Jesus, sent him to bless you, in turning away every one of you from his iniquities.

---Acts 3:22-26 (KJV)

Scriptures definition of "pure religion":

(26) If any man thinketh himself to be religious, while he bridleth not his tongue but deceiveth his heart, this man's religion is vain. **(27)** Pure religion and undefiled before our God and Father is this, to visit the fatherless and widows in their affliction, *and* to keep oneself unspotted from the world.

---James 1:26-27 (ASV)

Are we "unspotted from the world" or have we "blended or mixed" the world's ways with the Father's Ways?

Holy Days Observations (con't)

Since "blending" or "mixing" of religious beliefs is not a new concept, man has come up with an official name for this process: religious syncretism. [Syncretism as defined by the American Heritage Dictionary is the reconciliation or fusion of differing systems of belief. This is most evident in the areas of philosophy and religion, and usually results in a new teaching or belief system. Obviously, this can be very dangerous to Biblical Christianity.

Religious syncretism often takes place when foreign beliefs are introduced to an indigenous belief system and the teachings are blended. The new, heterogeneous religion then takes a shape of its own. This has been seen most clearly in Roman Catholic missionary history. Take, for example, the Roman Catholic Church's proselytization of animistic South America: Threatened with the fear of death, natives were baptized into the church by the tens of thousands without any preaching of the Gospel whatsoever; former temples were razed, with Catholic shrines and chapels built on the same spot; natives were allowed to substitute praying to saints instead of gods of water, earth and air, and replaced their former idols with new images of the Roman Catholic church. Yet, the animistic religion the natives had formerly practiced was never fully replaced--it was adapted into Catholic teachings, and this new belief system was allowed to flourish.

More recently, religious syncretism can be seen in such religious systems as the New Age, Hinduism, Unitarianism, and Christian Science. These religions are a blending of multiple different belief systems, and are even now continually evolving as the philosophies of mankind rise and fall in popularity.

Holy Days Observations (con't)

Therein lies the problem, for syncretism relies on the whim of man, not the standard of Scripture. The Bible makes it very clear what true religion is. Think on just a few things stated in Scripture: "Love the Lord your God with all your heart and with all your soul and with all your mind" (Deuteronomy 6:5; Matthew 22:37); "Jesus replied, 'I am the way and the truth and the life. No one comes to the Father except through me'" (John 14:6); and "Jesus did many other miraculous signs in the presence of his disciples, which are not recorded in this book. But these are written that you may believe that Jesus is the Christ, the Son of God, and that by believing you may have life in his name" (John 20:31-32).

Religious syncretism is simply not compatible with true Christianity. In fact, any modification to Biblical law and principle for the sake of a better religion is heresy (Revelation 22:18-19).] {36}

Conclusions

After reading the history, origins and descriptions of the modern Christian holidays and Biblical Holy Days, we are wondering what conclusions **you** might have reached.

If you are like us, our first question was, "How do the Biblical Feasts apply to us today?" Our conclusion on this question is that we, as believers in the one true God of Israel and His Son, Yeshua, are adopted (grafted) into the House of Israel. Therefore, we are also members of the Father's Household. As members of His household, what does he expect from us?

We have determined from scriptural and historical accounts the intensity of the Father's wrath for disobedience to His word and instructions. Time after time, mankind has tried to "improvise" by adding to or taking away from the instructions of YHWH.

Some of the conclusions we have come to...

1.) Do not add to or diminish from his commandments and observe them.

> **(28)** Observe and hear all these words which I command thee, that it may go well with thee, and with thy children after thee for ever, when thou doest *that which is* good and right in the sight of the LORD thy God. **(29)** When the LORD thy God shall cut off the nations from before thee, whither thou goest to possess them, and thou succeedest them, and dwellest in their land; **(30)** Take heed to thyself that thou be not snared by following them, after that they be destroyed from before thee; and that thou enquire not after their gods, saying, How did these nations serve their

Conclusions (con't)

gods? even so will I do likewise. **(31)** Thou shalt not do so unto the LORD thy God: for every abomination to the LORD, which he hateth, have they done unto their gods; for even their sons and their daughters they have burnt in the fire to their gods. **(32)** What thing soever I command you, observe to do it: thou shalt not add thereto, nor diminish from it.

---Deuteronomy 12:28-32 (KJV)

There are numerous accounts of His wrath to disobedience as our examples:

The golden calf – **Exodus 32** (outlined earlier, pgs. 3-6)

Offering of strange fire - **Leviticus 10:1-2** And Nadab and Abihu, the sons of Aaron, took either of them his censer, and put fire therein, and put incense thereon, and offered strange fire before the LORD, which he commanded them not. And there went out fire from the LORD, and devoured them, and they died before the LORD.

Multiple acts of disobedience and their results are recorded in the books of the prophets and in 1 & 2 Kings and 1 & 2 Chronicles.

These are only a few instances!

***Conclusions** (con't)*

(13) Yet the LORD testified against Israel, and against Judah, by all the prophets, *and by* all the seers, saying, Turn ye from your evil ways, and keep my commandments *and* my statutes, according to all the law which I commanded your fathers, and which I sent to you by my servants the prophets. **(14)** Notwithstanding they would not hear, but hardened their necks, like to the neck of their fathers, that did not believe in the LORD their God. **(15)** And they rejected his statutes, and his covenant that he made with their fathers, and his testimonies which he testified against them; and they followed **vanity**, and **became vain**, and went after the heathen that *were* round about them, *concerning* whom the LORD had charged them, that they should not do like them. **(16)** And they left all the commandments of the LORD their God, and made them molten images, *even* two calves, and made a grove, and worshipped all the host of heaven, and served Baal. **(17)** And they caused their sons and their daughters to pass through the fire, and used divination and enchantments, and sold themselves to do evil in the sight of the LORD, to provoke him to anger. **(18)** Therefore the LORD was very angry with Israel, and removed them out of his sight: there was none left but the tribe of Judah only. **(19)** Also Judah kept not the commandments of the LORD their God, but walked in the statutes of Israel which they made. **(20)** And the LORD rejected all the seed of Israel, and afflicted them, and delivered them into the hand of

Conclusions (con't)

spoilers, until he had cast them out of his sight.

---2 Kings 17:13-20 (KJV)

2.) YHWH is a jealous God.

3.) Have no other gods before Him.

(1) Then God spoke all these words: **(2)** "I am the LORD your God who brought you out of the land of Egypt, out of the house of slavery. **(3)** You are to have no other gods besides me. **(4)** "You are not to make for yourselves an idol, or any likeness of what is in heaven above, or on earth below, or in the water under the earth. **(5)** You are not to bow down to them in worship or serve them; because I, the LORD your God, am a jealous God, punishing the children for the iniquity of the parents, to the third and fourth generations of those who hate me, **(6)** but showing gracious love to the thousandth generation of those who love me and keep my commandments.

---Exodus 20:1-6 (ISV)

4.) YHWH never changes.

(6) "Because I the LORD don't change; therefore you children of Jacob, aren't destroyed." **(7)** "Even since the time of your ancestors you have turned away from my decrees and haven't kept them. Return to me and I'll return to you," says the LORD of the Heavenly Armies. "But you ask, 'How will we return?'

---Malachi 3:6-7 (ISV)

Conclusions (con't)

5.) YHWH and Yeshua are one.

(30) I and *my* Father are one.

---John 10:30 (KJV)

6.) Yeshua does the will of YHWH, His Father.

(30) I can of mine own self do nothing: as I hear, I judge: and my judgment is just; because I seek not mine own will, but the will of the Father which hath sent me.

---John 5:30 (KJV)

(28) So Jesus told them, "When you have lifted up the Son of Man, then you will know that I AM, and that I do nothing on my own authority. Instead, I speak only what the Father has taught me. **(29)** Moreover, the one who sent me is with me. He has never left me alone because I always do what pleases him."

---John 8:28-29 (ISV)

We know through scripture that the commandments of YHWH are also the commandments of Yeshua. They are one and the same. They share the same will. Our Heavenly Father did not have a plan A, B or C when He set the world and heavens in motion. He is the all seeing and almighty God of Creation. He created us and His world with one plan in mind. He has never altered this plan. He will see it accomplished in His due time.

Conclusions (con't)

(11) so will my message be that goes out of my mouth–it won't return to me empty. Instead, it will accomplish what I desire, and achieve the purpose for which I sent it.

---Isaiah 55:11 (ISV)

(14) I, the LORD have spoken. It will happen, because I'm going to do it. I won't hold back, have compassion, or change my mind. They'll judge you according to your ways and deeds,' declares the Lord GOD."

.

---Ezekiel 24:14 (ISV)

Our goal as His children and Yeshua's followers are to imitate Yeshua in seeking YHWH's will. How do we do this? Keep and do His commandments **with** the faith that He keeps His promises. This is the saving faith of Abraham, believe in YHWH's promises and do his commandments because of our love for Him and Yeshua.

7.) **We are told repeatedly throughout scripture by YHWH and Yeshua to keep and do the commandments. These are just a few:**

(6) And shewing mercy unto thousands of them that love me, and keep my commandments.

---Exodus 20:6 (KJV)

(31) Therefore shall ye keep my commandments, and do them: I am Jehovah.

---Leviticus 22:31 (ASV)

Conclusions (con't)

(3) "If you live by my statutes, obey my commands, and observe them, **(4)** then I'll send your rain in its season so that the land will yield its produce and the trees of the field will yield their fruit.

---Leviticus 26:3-4 (ISV)

(29) Oh that there were such a heart in them, that they would fear me, and keep all my commandments always, that it might be well with them, and with their children for ever!

---Deuteronomy 5:29 (ASV)

(14) If you will live life my way, keeping my statutes and my commands, just like your father David did, I'll also increase the length of your life."

---1 Kings 3:14 (ISV)

(13) Yet the LORD testified against Israel, and against Judah, by all the prophets, *and by* all the seers, saying, Turn ye from your evil ways, and keep my commandments *and* my statutes, according to all the law which I commanded your fathers, and which I sent to you by my servants the prophets.

---2 Kings 17:13 (KJV)

Conclusions (con't)

> **(30)** If his children forsake my law, And walk not in mine ordinances; **(31)** If they break my statutes, And keep not my commandments; **(32)** Then will I visit their transgression with the rod, And their iniquity with stripes.
>
> **--Psalms 89:30-32 (ASV)**

> **(1)** My son, forget not my law; but let thine heart keep my commandments: **(2)** For length of days, and long life, and peace, shall they add to thee. **(3)** Let not mercy and truth forsake thee: bind them about thy neck; write them upon the table of thine heart: **(4)** So shalt thou find favour and good understanding in the sight of God and man. **(5)** Trust in the LORD with all thine heart; and lean not unto thine own understanding. **(6)** In all thy ways acknowledge him, and he shall direct thy paths. **(7)** Be not wise in thine own eyes: fear the LORD, and depart from evil.
>
> **---Proverbs 3:1-7 (KJV)**

How many times do we think we are wise in our own eyes? Are we wise in YHWH's eyes, though?

> **(1)** Hear, ye children, the instruction of a father, and attend to know understanding. **(2)** For I give you good doctrine, forsake ye not my law.
>
> **---Proverbs 4:1-2 (KJV)**

Conclusions (con't)

(1) My son, keep my words, and lay up my commandments with thee. **(2)** Keep my commandments, and live; and my law as the apple of thine eye. **(3)** Bind them upon thy fingers, write them upon the table of thine heart.

---Proverbs 7:1-2 (KJV)

(3) "So I turned my attention to the Lord God, seeking him in prayer and supplication, accompanied with fasting, sackcloth, and ashes. **(4)** I prayed to the LORD my God, confessing and saying: Lord! Great and awesome God, who keeps his covenant and gracious love for those who love him and obey his commandments,

---Daniel 9:3-4 (ISV)

(15) "If you love me, keep my commandments.

---John 14:15 (ISV)

(21) The person who has my commandments and keeps them is the one who loves me. The one who loves me will be loved by my Father, and I, too, will love him and reveal myself to him."

---John 14:21 (ISV)

(10) If ye keep my commandments, ye shall abide in my love; even as I have kept my Father's commandments, and abide in his love.

---John 15:10 (ASV)

Summary

So, in summary, each of us has been given free will from our birth. YHWH has given this to us. He does not want robot followers. He wants loving children who obey Him because we love Him!

We are given our instruction manual on how to live as members of the Father's Household, His Scriptures. To become a member of His House is our choice. Once we are adopted into His family, we must make choices as to whose will we are going to follow, His or our own.

Our lives are influenced by Satan and the world around us. Our choices in this life will determine the blessings we receive during our lifetime and will also affect our eternity. If we can not figure out how He wants us to worship Him in this lifetime, how will we know what is expected of us in His Kingdom for eternity?

Satan has played a major role in changing the holy festivals of our Father. He has encouraged man to incorporate "the ways of the heathen" into our holy days, resulting in the mixing or blending of Yeshua and paganism. The Father is very specific in His chosen people being Holy, *Kadosh*, which means Set-Apart. If we observe the festivals of the world (which have pagan roots) that the masses observe, are we truly set-apart for service unto the one true God of Israel? If He declared that the ways of the heathen were abominations to Him all those years ago and scripture tells us HE CHANGES NOT, why do we assume He is accepting of these observances now?

Summary (con't)

(9) He that turneth away his ear from hearing the law, Even his prayer is an abomination.

---Proverbs 28:9 (ASV)

(10) Hear the word of the LORD, ye rulers of Sodom; give
ear unto the law of our God, ye people of Gomorrah. **(11)**
To what purpose *is* the multitude of your sacrifices unto
me? saith the LORD: I am full of the burnt offerings of
rams, and the fat of fed beasts; and I delight not in the
blood of bullocks, or of lambs, or of he goats. **(12)** When
ye come to appear before me, who hath required this at
your hand, to tread my courts? **(13)** Bring no more vain
oblations; incense is an abomination unto me; the new
moons and sabbaths, the calling of assemblies, I cannot
away with; *it is* iniquity, even the solemn meeting. **(14)**
Your new moons and your appointed feasts my soul hateth:
they are a trouble unto me; I am weary to bear *them*. **(15)**
And when ye spread forth your hands, I will hide mine eyes
from you: yea, when ye make many prayers, I will not hear:
your hands are full of blood.

---Isaiah 1:10-15 (KJV)

The folks in the above scriptures were "going through the motions" of worshipping the Father by offering sacrifices, burning incense, observing the new moons and Sabbaths, observing the appointed feasts as the Father had instructed, but they were being disobedient to Him in their everyday lives,

Summary (con't)

living in iniquity. Iniquity is defined in Strong's Concordance #G458 as: From G459; illegality, that is, violation of law or (generally) wickedness: - iniquity, X transgress (-ion of) the law, unrighteousness.

> **(4)** Whosoever committeth sin transgresseth also the law: for sin is the transgression of the law.
>
> **---1 John 3:4 (KJV)**

Iniquity = transgression of the Law (or lawlessness, without law)
Sin = transgression of the Law (or lawlessness, without law)

If you should choose to celebrate and honor the festivals of the Father instead of the traditional holidays we have all grown up observing, you will definitely come under scrutiny, condemnation and ridicule from your friends and family. This will make your choice harder, but you must choose who you will serve, YHWH or man. When these times come, remember the following words of Yeshua:

> **(51)** "Do you think that I came to bring peace on earth? Not at all, I tell you, but rather division! **(52)** From now on, five people in one household will be divided, three against two and two against three. **(53)** They will be divided father against son, son against father, mother against daughter, daughter against mother, mother-in-law against daughter-in-law, and daughter-in-law against mother-in-law."
>
> **---Luke 12:51-53 (ISV)**

Summary *(con't)*

> **(34)** "Do not think that I came to bring peace on earth. I did not come to bring peace but a sword! **(35)** I came to turn 'a man against his father, a daughter against her mother, and a daughter-in-law against her mother-in-law. **(36)** A person's enemies will include members of his own family.' **(37)** "The one who loves his father or mother more than me isn't worthy of me, and the one who loves a son or daughter more than me isn't worthy of me.
>
> **---Matthew 10:34-37 (ISV)**

We cannot follow both man's doctrine and Yeshua and YHWH's doctrines (***unless*** they are one in the same) **or** be in the middle of the road. We must keep in mind that man has added traditions and celebrations (*both* Christian and Hebrew) to the Father's designated festivals. We should pray for the Spirit to guide us and help us to have a discerning spirit to discern the pure from the mixed.

We must make the choice and not comprise.

Summary (con't)

(14) Now therefore fear the LORD, and serve him in sincerity and in truth: and put away the gods which your fathers served on the other side of the flood, and in Egypt; and serve ye the LORD. **(15)** And if it seem evil unto you to serve the LORD, choose you this day whom ye will serve; whether the gods which your fathers served that *were* on the other side of the flood, or the gods of the Amorites, in whose land ye dwell: but as for me and my house, we will serve the LORD.

---Joshua 24:14-15 (KJV)

(19) I call heaven and earth to witness against you this day, that I have set before thee life and death, the blessing and the curse: therefore choose life, that thou mayest live, thou and thy seed;

---Deuteronomy 30:19 (ASV)

(24) "No one can serve two masters, because either he will hate one and love the other, or be loyal to one and despise the other. You cannot serve God and riches!"

---Matthew 6:24 (ISV)

(15) I know thy works, that thou art neither cold nor hot: I would thou wert cold or hot. **(16)** So because thou art lukewarm, and neither hot nor cold, I will spew thee out of my mouth.

---Revelation 3:15-16 (ASV)

Summary (con't)

Our fellow brothers and sisters before us have given the greatest examples of how NOT to live as children in our Father's Household. One of our favorites is from Ezekiel. Please read the entire chapter when you have time.

> **(17)** Son of man, when the house of Israel dwelt in their own land, they defiled it by their own way and by their doings: their way was before me as the uncleanness of a removed woman. **(18)** Wherefore I poured my fury upon them for the blood that they had shed upon the land, and for their idols *wherewith* they had polluted it: **(19)** And I scattered them among the heathen, and they were dispersed through the countries: according to their way and according to their doings I judged them. **(20)** And when they entered unto the heathen, whither they went, they profaned my holy name, when they said to them, These *are* the people of the LORD, and are gone forth out of his land. **(21)** But I had pity for mine holy name, which the house of Israel had profaned among the heathen, whither they went. **(22)** Therefore say unto the house of Israel, Thus saith the Lord GOD; I do not *this* for your sakes, O house of Israel, but for mine holy name's sake, which ye have profaned among the heathen, whither ye went. **(23)** And I will sanctify my great name, which was profaned among the heathen, which ye have profaned in the midst of them; and the heathen shall know that I *am* the LORD, saith the Lord GOD, when I shall be sanctified in you before their eyes. **(24)** For I will take you from

Summary (con't)

among the heathen, and gather you out of all countries, and will bring you into your own land. **(25)** Then will I sprinkle clean water upon you, and ye shall be clean: from all your filthiness, and from all your idols, will I cleanse you. **(26)** A new heart also will I give you, and a new spirit will I put within you: and I will take away the stony heart out of your flesh, and I will give you an heart of flesh. **(27)** And I will put my spirit within you, and cause you to walk in my statutes, and ye shall keep my judgments, and do *them*. **(28)** And ye shall dwell in the land that I gave to your fathers; and ye shall be my people, and I will be your God.

---Ezekiel 36:17-28 (KJV)

Summary *(con't)*

Our spiritual ancestors were taken into the Promised Land, the land of their inheritance (***our inheritance also***) and took on the ways of the heathen around them and developed their own ways instead of the Father's. They defiled the land and profaned the Father's holy name by their actions and their own way. We are sure that in their eyes they justified their behavior before each other, but they could not justify their way before their Creator and Deliverer! We must always remember that WE are not our own judge! YHWH alone has the right to judge us. He as Father created us and He as Savior shed His blood for our salvation. He alone grants grace and mercy and sees our hearts for what they truly are!

YHWH Himself states that His mercy and grace is extended NOT for Israel's sake (His Household's sake) but to sanctify His HOLY NAME'S SAKE so that the heathen will know that HE is the Elohim! Notice that here, in what we have called the Old Testament, He tells us that He will gather His people, cleanse them, give them a new heart and spirit, and will place His Spirit within them which will cause them to walk in His statutes and keep His judgments and DO them. Reminds us of the descending of the Holy Spirit, Ruach HaKodesh, during the time of Pentecost, does it not?

Summary *(con't)*

So, the choice is ours. Personally, we pray we never hear the following words from Yeshua, our Savior…

> **(8)** 'These people honor me with their lips, but their hearts are far from me. **(9)** Their worship of me is empty, because they teach human rules as doctrines.'"

---Matthew 15:8-9 (ISV)

> **(20)** Wherefore by their fruits ye shall know them. **(21)** Not every one that saith unto me, Master, Master, shall enter into the kingdom of heaven; but he that doeth the will of my Father which is in heaven. **(22)** Many will say to me in that day, Master, Master, have we not prophesied in thy name? and in thy name have cast out devils? and in thy name done many wonderful works? **(23)** And then will I profess unto them, I never knew you: depart from me, ye that work iniquity.

---Matthew 7:20-23 (KJV)

Summary (con't)

Instead we pray that we hear…

(21) …*Well done, thou good and faithful servant: thou hast been faithful over a few things, I will make thee ruler over many things: enter thou into the joy of thy lord.*

---Matthew 25:21 (KJV)

It is our choice!

Reference List

1. 'Strong's Concordance of the Bible' by James Strong, LL.D, S.T.D. Available through e-sword free Bible Study Software at: http://www.e-sword.net © 2000-2008 - Rick Meyers, Version 7.9.0.8
2. 'Feast of Trumpets (Christian holiday)', from Wikipedia, the free encyclopedia. Content from Wikipedia available under GFDL license, Version 1.2, November 2002 Copyright ©2000, 2001, and 2002. Page last modified April 10, 2008, at 21:56, by R'n'B, reverted edits by JonHarder; viewed May 20, 2008. Available at: http://en.wikipedia.org/wiki/Feast_of_Trumpets_%28Christian_holiday%29
3. 'Holiday', from The Free Dictionary by Farlex. The American Heritage® Dictionary of the English Language, Fourth Edition copyright ©2000 by Houghton Mifflin Company. Updated 2003. Published by Houghton Mifflin Company. All rights reserved; viewed May 22, 2008. Available at: http://www.thefreedictionary.com/holiday
4. Lew White, '*Fossilized Customs, The Pagan Origins of Popular Customs*', Strawberry Islands Messianic Publishing. Available from www.fossilizedcustoms.com
5. 'Epiphany', from Columbia Electronic Encyclopedia. Columbia University Press; viewed May 22, 2008. Available at: http://www/reference.com/browse/columbia/Epiphany
6. 'Questions and Answers about the Epiphany of our Lord', from Saint Paul's Lutheran Church, Kingsville, MD. Website last updated May 19, 2008; viewed May 22, 2008. Available at: http://www.stpaulskingsville.org/
7. 'Christian Holidays, Mardi Gras', from ReligionFacts ©2004-2008. Page published January 10, 2005, updated January 26, 2007; viewed May 23, 2008. Available at: http://www.religionfacts.com/christianity/holidays/mardi_gras.htm#3

Reference List (con't)

8. 'Easter', from University of Waterloo, 200 University Avenue West, Waterloo, Ontario, Canada N2L 3G1, 519-888-4567, http://www.uwaterloo.ca; viewed May 23, 2008. Available at: http://www.math.uwaterloo.ca/~rbutterw/essays/Easter
9. 'Easter is the Mother of Baal', from Bibleline Ministries™ Calvary Community Church by Dr. Hank Lindstrom; viewed June 17, 2008. Available at: http://www.biblelineministries.org/articles/basearch.php3?action=full&mainkey=EASTER+IS+THE+MOTHER+OF+BAAL&typed=Easter
10. Ecclesiastical History of England 5.23, quoted in "Easter Controversy," Catholic Encyclopedia
11. Valerie Moody, '*The Feasts of Adonai, Why Christians Should Look at the Biblical Feasts*', Gibbora Productions ©2002-2005. Available from www.vmoodyart.com or 806-791-2400
12. 'Virgo', from The Constellations by Richard Dibon-Smith; viewed June 16, 2008 Available at: http://www.dibonsmith.com/vir_con.htm
13. '*Langenscheidt Pocket Merriam-Webster Dictionary',* Merriam-Webster, Incorported, Springfield Massachusetts, U.S.A. ©1994 & Lngenshceidt Publishers, Inc. New York ©1997, p. 643.
14. 'The Early Church and the Festival of Unleavened Bread', from www.BibleResearch.org by B. L. Cocherell, file b5w49; viewed June 16, 2008. Available at: http://www.bibleresearch.org/observancebook5/b5249.html
15. 'The Day of Trumpets', from www.lastdaysmystery.info by Richard H. Perry; viewed May 23, 2008. Available at: http://www.lastdaysmystery.info/feast_of_trumpets.htm
16. Mike Evans, Jerusalem Prayer Team, email dated Dec. 2007. Please visit http://jerusalemprayerteam.org
17. 'Sunday', from Wikipedia. Page last modified May 20, 2008, at 11:13, by Tresiden, reverted edits by 203.87.64.221 to last version by RyanLupin; viewed May 21, 2008. Available at: http://en.wikipedia.org/wiki/Sunday

Reference List *(con't)*

18. 'Epiphany (holiday)', from Wikipedia. Page last modified May 18, 2008, at 14:39, by MishaPan; viewed May 21, 2008. Available at: http://en.wikipedia.org/wiki/Epiphany_%28holiday%29
19. 'Halloween', from Wikipedia. Page last modified May 21, 2008, at 16:29, by Razorflame, reverted edits by 69.67.80.23; viewed May 21, 2008. Available at: http://en.wikipedia.org/wiki/Halloween
20. 'Thanksgiving (United States)', from Wikipedia. Page last modified May 21, 2008, at 22:43, by Dicklyon, reverted 1 edit by 69.114.215.222 identified as vandalism to last revision by JMyrleFuller. (TW); viewed May 21, 2008. Available at: http://en.wikipedia.org/wiki/Thanksgiving_%28United_States%29
21. 'Christmas', from Wikipedia. Page last modified May 21, 2008, at 18:56, by Gurchzilla, reverted edits by 208.125.7.2 to last version by Tresiden); viewed May 21, 2008. Available at: http://en.wikipedia.org/wiki/Christmas
22. 'Sabbath in Christianity', from Wikipedia. Page last modified May 11, 2008, at 21:23, by John Bulten; viewed May 22, 2008. Available at: http://en.wikipedia.org/wiki/Sabbath_in_Christianity
23. 'Passover', from Wikipedia. Page last modified May 22, 2008, at 14:37, by SoLando, reverted edits by 70.105.62.208 to last version by ClueBot; viewed May 22, 2008. Available at: http://en.wikipedia.org/wiki/Passover
24. 'Sukkot', from Wikipedia. Page last modified May 21, 2008, at 19:39, by Elan26; viewed May 22, 2008. Available at: http://en.wikipedia.org/wiki/Sukkot
25. 'Feast of Tabernacles (Christian holiday)', from Wikipedia. Page last modified April 8, 2008, at 01:06, by 58.107.66.59; viewed May 22, 2008. Available at: http://en.wikipedia.org/wiki/Feast_of_Tabernacles%2C_Christian

Reference List (con't)

26. 'Holy Day', from The Free Dictionary by Farlex. The American Heritage® Dictionary of the English Language, Fourth Edition ©2000 by Houghton Mifflin Company. Updated 2003. Published by Houghton Mifflin Company. All rights reserved; viewed May 22, 2008. Available at: http://www.thefreedictionary.com/holy+day
27. 'Christian Holidays, Ash Wednesday, from ReligionFacts ©2004-2008. Page published January 4, 2005, updated January 26, 2007; viewed May 23, 2008. Available at: http://www.religionfacts.com/christianity/holidays/ash_wednesday.htm
28. 'Christian Holidays, Lent, from ReligionFacts ©2004-2008. Page published March 17, 2004, updated March 8, 2006; viewed May 23, 2008. Available at: http://www.religionfacts.com/christianity/holidays/lent.htm
29. 'Christian Holidays, Valentine's Day, from ReligionFacts ©2004-2008. Page published February 10, 2005, updated January 31, 2007; viewed May 23, 2008. Available at: http://www.religionfacts.com/christianity/holidays/valentines_day.htm
30. 'Christian Holidays, Palm Sunday, from ReligionFacts ©2004-2008. Page published March 13, 2005; viewed May 23, 2008. Available at: http://www.religionfacts.com/christianity/holidays/palm_sunday.htm
31. 'Christian Holidays, Easter, from ReligionFacts ©2004-2008. Page published March 17, 2004, updated March 7, 2005; viewed May 23, 2008. Available at: http://www.religionfacts.com/christianity/holidays/easter.htm
32. 'Christian Holidays, St. Patrick's Day, from ReligionFacts ©2004-2008. Page published January 11, 2005, updated April 11, 2006; viewed May 23, 2008. Available at: http://www.religionfacts.com/christianity/holidays/st_patricks_day.htm
33. 'Christian Holidays, Thanksgiving, from ReligionFacts ©2004-2008. Page published November 22, 2004, updated October 13, 2005; viewed May 23, 2008. Available at: http://www.religionfacts.com/christianity/holidays/thanksgiving.htm

Reference List (con't)

34. 'Christian Holidays, St. Andrew's Day, from ReligionFacts ©2004-2008. Page published November 27, 2004; viewed May 23, 2008. Available at: http://www.religionfacts.com/christianity/holidays/st_andrews_day.htm
35. 'Christian Holidays, Christmas', from ReligionFacts ©2004-2008. Page published March 17, 2004, updated December 5, 2007; viewed May 23, 2008. Available at: http://www.religionfacts.com/christianity/holidays/christmas.htm
36. 'What is religious syncretism?', from gotQuestions?org ©2002-2008 Got Questions Ministries. Viewed July 8, 2008. Available at: http://www.gotquestions.org/
37. 'I & II Maccabee', from The Common Man's Prospective ©1999-2008. Viewed January 14, 2009. Available at: http://www.ecmarsh.com/lxx/I%20Maccabees/index.htm
38. 'Saturnalia', from Wikipedia. Page last modified January 7, 2009, at 6:08; viewed January 15, 2009. Available at: http://en.wikipedia.org/wiki/Saturnalia

All scriptural references were taken from:

- Liberty University's "The King James Study Bible"
- e-Sword Bible Study Software, available free at www.e-sword.net

Other excellent sources of research material on the Festivals and Hebraic Roots of Christianity can be found at:

- Living River Ministry & Radio Station, www.kdshfm.com
- Eddie Chumney, www.hebroots.org
- John Garr, http://www.hebraiccommunity.org
- Rico Cortez, www.wisdomintorah.com
- Monte Judah, www.lionlamb.net
- Bill Cloud, www.billcloud.org
- Brad Scott, www.wildbranch.org
- Lew White, www.fossilizedcustoms.com
- Valerie Moody, www.vmoodyart.com
- Tony Robinson, www.restorationoftorah.org
- Michael Rood, http://michaelrood.tv/
- Various Teachers, http://www.hebraicrootsnetwork.com/

After Thoughts

While scanning my email around the time of Passover, I ran across an interesting article forwarded to me by a dear friend. The article was sent as a subscription called, "First Fruits Update", from the First Fruits of Zion ministry out of Marshfield, MO founded by Michael Boaz. The update referred to a recent article in *Time* magazine entitled, "Ten Ideas That Are Changing the World". Low and behold, the tenth "idea" mentioned was "Re-Judaizing Jesus". With today's self-serving, push anything "religious" out of our way, society I was surprised to see this one on the list!

First Fruits of Zion is focused on proclaiming the Torah and its way of life to today's believers in the one true God of Israel. They prepared a short news story in press-release format to help folks reach out to our fellow brothers and sisters during Passover. The news release was entitled, "Re-Judaizing Jesus: Christians Returning to Jewish Roots". One comment especially caught my eye. The comment was made by author and historian D. Thomas Lancaster, who currently leads a messianic synagogue in Hudson, Wisconsin with a congregation made up of more non-Jewish than Jewish members. His statement was, "Jesus is beginning to be re-contextualized back into His proper cultural and historical setting. There are a lot of Christians who place a high value on biblical authority, and they're serious enough to re-examine their own practices for authenticity." This statement impressed me! This is exactly the point in our walk that my husband and I reached many years ago...to re-examine our own practices for authenticity! Shouldn't this be every believer's earthly quest in regard to their relationship with their Creator and Father?

After Thoughts (con't)

The press release then went on to say that a recent cover story in *Time* magazine (March 24, 2008) agrees. It noted that the ten ideas listed, "Re-Judaizing Jesus" as number ten, will have an impact, "more than money, more than politics…" Lancaster commented that he believes this to be very true and found *Time's* assessment amusing but not surprising. "When you read the biblical prophecies of Revelation, Daniel and others within their Jewish contexts, it becomes pretty clear that when Jesus returns, He'll still be Jewish. That's bound to surprise some people."

In reading the *Time* article itself, I must disagree with a statement made by the author, David Van Biema. Mr. Van Biema stated the following, "The shift came in stages: first brute acceptance that Jesus was born a Jew and did Jewish things; then admission that he and his interpreter Paul saw themselves as Jews even while founding what became another faith…" I take issue with his idea that Yeshua and Paul founded another faith. Scripture tells us very plainly that there is but **one** faith!

A quote from Amy-Jill Levine, a Vanderbilt University New Testament scholar, does ring true, however, "if you get the [Jewish] context wrong, you will certainly get Jesus wrong." If we as modern-day believers don't understand Yeshua's Jewish (Hebraic) walk, how can we truly walk in His footsteps? After all, **His** footsteps will lead us down that straight and narrow path, not man's that can lead us down a multitude of doctrinal theology and beliefs.

"Now it will come about that in the last days... many people will come and say, 'Come, let us go up to the mountain of the LORD, to the house of the God of Jacob; that He may teach us

After Thoughts (con't)

concerning His ways, and that we may walk in His paths.' For the Torah will go forth from Zion, and the word of the Lord from Jerusalem." (Isaiah 2:2–3)

First Fruits of Zion press release may be found at: www.ffoz.org or www.torahclub.org
Time article may be found at:
http://www.time.com/time/specials/2007/article/0,28804,1720049_1720050_1721663,00.html

Scriptures for Thought

(4) And Jesus answered and said unto them, Take heed that no man deceive you.

---Matthew 24:4 (KJV)

(6) My people are destroyed because they lack knowledge of me. Because you rejected that knowledge, I will reject you as a priest for me. Since you forget the Law of your God, I will also forget your children.

---Hosea 4:6 (ISV)

(28) Observe and hear all these words which I command thee, that it may go well with thee, and with thy children after thee forever, when thou doest *that which is* good and
right in the sight of the LORD thy God. **(29)** When the
LORD thy God shall cut off the nations from before thee, whither thou goest to possess them, and thou succeedest
them, and dwellest in their land; **(30)** Take heed to thyself
that thou be not snared by following them, after that they be destroyed from before thee; and that thou inquire not after their gods, saying, How did these nations serve their
gods? even so will I do likewise. **(31)** Thou shalt not do so
unto the LORD thy God: for every abomination to the LORD, which he hateth, have they done unto their gods; for even their sons and their daughters they have burnt in
the fire to their gods. **(32)** What thing soever command
you, observe to do it: thou shalt not add thereto, nor diminish from it.

---Deuteronomy 12:28-32 (KJV)

Scriptures for Thought (con't)

YHWH's Word commands us not to be like the pagans and heathens. He commands us to worship Him in spirit and in truth and not to worship Him as the pagans worship their gods.

Closing Blessings

(24) YHWH bless thee, and keep thee: **(25)** YHWH make His face shine upon thee, and be gracious unto thee: **(26)** YHWH lift up His countenance upon thee, and give thee peace.

---Numbers 6:24-26 (KJV)

May YHWH through His Set-Apart Spirit guide you to His truth and wisdom. May He give you discernment and understanding of His ways, and may you strive to do what is pleasing in His eyes.

Blessings & Peace (Shalom)!

Made in the USA
Monee, IL
12 October 2022